Revitalizing the Twentieth-Century Church

Revitalizing the Twentieth-Century Church

by

Norman Shawchuck
and
Lloyd M. Perry

MOODY PRESS
CHICAGO

© 1982 by
THE MOODY BIBLE INSTITUTE
OF CHICAGO

Paperback Edition, 1986

All rights reserved. No part of this book may be reproduced in any form without permission in writing from the publisher, except in the case of brief quotations embodied in critical articles or reviews.

All Scripture quotations, except those noted otherwise, are from the *New American Standard Bible,* © 1960, 1962, 1963, 1968, 1971, 1972, 1973, 1975, and 1977 by The Lockman Foundation, and are used by permission.

The use of selected references from various versions of the Bible in this publication does not imply publisher endorsement of the versions in their entirety.

This book is a sequel to *Getting the Church on Target* by Lloyd M. Perry (Chicago: Moody, 1977). It builds upon and expands the ideas in that earlier book.

Library of Congress Cataloging in Publication Data

Shawchuck, Norman, 1935-
  Revitalizing the twentieth-century church.

  Bibliography: p. 181
  Includes index.
  1. Church renewal. I. Perry, Lloyd Merle.
II. Title.
BV600.2.S49   253   81-16974
ISBN 0-8024-7317-2   AACR2
ISBN 0-8024-7318-0 (pbk.)

5 6 7 Printing/BB/Year 91 90 89

Printed in the United States of America

Contents

CHAPTER	PAGE
Introduction	7
1. Planning to Make Your Visions Come True: Mission Clarification and Congregational Assessment	13
2. Planning to Make Your Visions Come True: Goal Setting, Implementation, and Evaluation	31
3. Organizing for Action	47
4. Developing Church Leadership	59
5. Financial Aspects of Revitalization	75
6. Relational Aspects of Revitalization	87
7. Missional Aspects of Revitalization	105
8. Proclamational Aspects of Revitalization	113
9. Theological Reflection on Church Revitalization Processes	137
Conclusion	151
Appendix A	155
Appendix B	159
Appendix C	163
Bibliography	181

Introduction

> There is a wide-spread unrest and dissatisfaction in today's church due to the fact that the bulk of the membership, the laity, has traditionally been regarded as inferior to the clergy. But such division of church membership into two classes is quite removed from the intent of Scripture. The recovery of the laity will have a positive effect upon the recovery of the church.[1]

This book is about revitalizing a local church. You have been praying that your church may experience new life, and you are searching for ways to make that happen.

This book was written just for you. You may be uncomfortable with some of what we say, and you may argue with some of our ideas. But WE DARE YOU TO READ THIS BOOK FROM BEGINNING TO END. If you are not absolutely satisfied with your church as it is now, if there is still room for improvement and growth, if you dream of a broader and more exciting ministry, this book is for you.

It was not written to confirm what you already know. It was written to make you more effective. In order to be more effective, you must grow. In order to grow you must learn new ideas and models for ministry. New ideas and models, just because they are new, cause some discomfort. But it is a discomfort that leads to growth and effectiveness. Without tension and experimentation there is no growth.

This is not our last word on revitalization. It is, however, an essential beginning. As you read this book please remember this: if we discussed only that which you already know, or if we said only that with which you already fully agree, there would be nothing for you to gain from this book.

Your openness, and therefore your ability, to hear what Christ has to say is always affected by what you expect to hear Him say. In fact, becoming very familiar with Christ's Word always brings with it the danger of reading and hearing the Word through a set of filters that filter in only that which Christ is expected to say and filter out anything unexpected. This results in tunnel vision, seeing in the Word only that which fits preconceived notions of what Christ would ever say to the church. Pastors in particular confront yet another danger. Having come to see only what they expect to see in the Word, they develop a tunnel approach in their preaching. They preach and teach the same limited themes and doctrines over and over again.

It is interesting that that tunnel vision allows pastors to see the faults and omissions in the preaching and leadership of other pastors, but it completely blinds them to their own. To verify this one need only listen to the conversations of a few groups of pastors as they discuss other groups of pastors. One group says of another, "They don't even preach salvation. The social gospel will never be sufficient to save the world." But another group says, "All they are concerned about is getting people to the altar. Won't they ever learn that faith without works is dead?" Each group identifies the tunnel vision of the other, but fails to see the narrow perspective of its own position.

The one group never gets its folk to first base. To those pastors Christ is saying, "Most certainly I tell you, people must be born again, for unless they repent they will perish" (see John 3:7 and Luke 13:3). The other group never gets its folk beyond first base. To that group of pastors Christ is saying, "Move beyond the elementary teachings about Christ. Lead My people into a mature faith. Do not bring them back again and again to the altar for repentance. Teach them something more than baptism, the laying on of hands, the resurrection, and eternal judgment. By now the people whom I have put in your care should be mature Christians, effective ministers in their own right, but because you have kept them at the beginner's level regarding all that God expects of them they still need milk and cannot digest solid food" (see Heb. 5:12—6:2).

Pity the people whose pastor does not teach them all that Christ has to say regarding the plan of salvation, for they never have the will to serve Christ fully. Pity the people whose pastor does not teach them all that Christ has to say about mature Christian responsibility, for they never find the strength to serve Christ fully.

Bringing God's people to the place where they can serve Christ fully, where they can do all that He asks of them—that is revitalization. That is what this book is all about.

Have we overemphasized our point? Before you decide, let us tell you about a young Nazarene pastor who was a student in one of our classes at Trinity Evangelical Divinity School. This pastor had been in his present charge for three years. The church itself is over twenty years old and has been blessed with a succession of fine pastors. Our student, however, spent a good deal of time complaining about the "do-nothing" congregation and their low spiritual vitality.

At one point the class challenged his consistently negative view of his congregation, asking him what kind of leadership he had been offering for three years, and whether his own leadership and preaching might not have had a great deal to do with the condition of the congregation. His response was, "I've spent all of my time for the past three years trying to get these people saved, and I haven't even been able to do that yet!"

"Do you mean to tell us," the class asked, "that these good folk have been members of the Nazarene church, sitting under the ministry of concerned Nazarene pastors for twenty years, and they're still not even saved?"

"Until I personally see each one of them on their knees at the altar, and hear them repenting of their sins, I will never be sure they have been saved."

Now, let us assume that every pastor of that congregation felt the same way, and that each spent three or four years of ministry there calling those people to repentance. It does not take much imagination to assume that after a while the congregation would come to believe that repentance is all there is to the Christian life. Is it any wonder that it is a "do-nothing" church?

It is precisely that kind of clergy mentality that Paul addressed when he said not to lay again a foundation of repentance (Heb. 6:1).

In this book we do not intend to lay a foundation of repentance. Neither will we talk about baptism, laying on of hands, the resurrection of the dead, or eternal judgment. We assume that you already know those to be elementary (that is, they must come first) to the Christian faith.

Having made that assumption, we will talk about how you can enable your people to press on to maturity—to find that extra ingredient that still seems to be lacking in the life of your church. We will assume that you and the pastors who preceded you already know how and have succeeded in bringing your congregation (or a group within it) to first base, and, having made that assumption, we will present strategies for getting them to second, third, and finally to begin scoring in a way your church is not now doing in its ministries.

Throughout this book we will be advocating an intentional approach to ministry. A church can hardly hope for new life when it muddles along from Sunday to Sunday repeatedly calling the faithful to repentance. There is an entire life and ministry beyond repentance. It is there that revitalization is experienced. It is there that God meets and leads his people.

This book will stress the idea that taking an intentional, active approach to ministry will give the Holy Spirit something to talk to the church about. Even the Holy Spirit cannot speak to an empty vacuum.

This is a book for church leaders who want to be effective. James Burns says, "All leadership is goal-oriented. The failure to set goals is a sign of faltering leadership. Successful leadership points in a direction; it is also the vehicle of continuing and achieving purpose."[2] We agree, and therefore present in this book tried and proved methods for drawing both church leaders and members into the shaping of purpose for the church's ministry. In doing this we are not taking away anything that your church already has: prayer, prophecy, or preaching. Rather, we are adding to it to give it more power, spirit, and direction. To that end we send forth this book.

NOTES

1. Lloyd M. Perry, *Getting the Church on Target* (Chicago: Moody, 1977), p. 105.
2. James McGregor Burns, *Leadership* (New York: Harper & Row, 1978), p. 455.

1

Planning to Make Your Visions Come True: Mission Clarification and Congregational Assessment

Proverbs 29:18 declares, "Where there is no vision the people perish" (KJV*). That is where we must begin in talking about the revitalization of a local church.

Visions hold one thing in common with wishes and dreams in that they are images of a desired condition. A vision, however, differs from wishes and dreams in certain important respects.

A wish is an image of something a person would like to see happen, but it is believed to be beyond his ability to accomplish, and no one else cares enough about it to do it for him. Therefore, people often wish for impossible situations. "I wish I were twenty-one years old instead of only twelve," or "I wish Christmas would come every day." Having wished for something impossible, the responsiblity for the magic needed to provide the wish is placed upon far distant objects: "Star light, star bright, how I wish upon a star tonight. . . ."

Persons who wish for everything usually expect nothing and therefore attach very little emotion to their wish-images. Because they are emotionally uninvolved in their wishes, they are willing to invest very little of themselves (time, effort, money, reputation) in turning the wish into reality. Why then do people wish at all? Because wishing is safe. They have no emotions or effort invested, and since they do not really expect them to happen in the first place, they will not be too disappointed when they do not happen.

A dream is also an image of something a person would like to

*King James Version.

see happen. It differs from a wish in that it carries with it a significant emotional experience. Because the emotions are linked to the dream, a person will feel the dream much more keenly and will spend a great deal more time pondering upon it than upon a mere wish. The boy may wish to be twenty-one, and then quickly forget the whole business as mother sets a dish of ice cream before him. Some years later, however, the same boy, having reached twenty-one, may lose his appetite completely as he dreams of being near the beautiful girl who smiled at him and touched his hand in chemistry lab last week.

A dream may occupy a great deal of time, thought, and emotional energy. In fact, it may become so powerful as to fill one's nocturnal images and then dominate one's days in the form of daydreams. A dream may cause joy or pain depending upon how one assesses the chances of the dream ever becoming reality.

In spite of all that, however, people often are willing to invest only mental-emotional energy in their dreams, and, like those who wish, will not invest the necessary time, effort, money, or reputation required to turn their dreams into reality.

A vision, like a wish, begins with an image of something the person or group would like to see happen, and, like a dream, excites all the emotions. But a vision goes beyond either a wish or a dream to "capture" the person. A person may "have" a wish or a dream. A vision, however, "has" the person. Having come under the control of the vision, a person will pay any price, to the point of death, to bring the vision into full reality.

In a real sense the person is always bigger than a wish, a dream that takes it source from the person's own being. A vision, however, is always larger than the person and takes its source from an external reality that is larger than the person.

One can tell whether a person or group is expressing a wish, a dream, or a vision by listening to their words and by observing their own reactions to and investments in the image they have described. Words alone are enough to substantiate a wish. Dreams can be substantiated by words and a strong emotional attachment. A vision, however, will align all of the person's words, emotions, and actions into a common quest to bring it into reality.

In Joel 2:28 the Lord promises that both dreams and visions

will be given to the congregation when the Spirit comes among the people. It is noteworthy that he said the old people would dream the dreams but the young people would see visions. Why that distinction? Because a vision demands one's strength, vigor, and vitality. The Lord is saying that dreams are the property of those whose strength and vitality is gone. He will give his visions to those who have the strength and energy to turn them into reality.

The tremendous effect of a vision upon a person or group is illustrated repeatedly in Scripture. In Isaiah 6, Isaiah tells us that he saw the Lord. Was it a vision, or was it merely a dream? Verse 5 lets us know that it was at least a dream (not a wish), for Isaiah attaches great emotion to what he saw. Verse 8, however, lets us know that it was more than simply a dream, for the experience captured him and impelled his life from that point on. "Here am I. Send me" is not the language of a dreamer, but a doer. A vision will always result in action! Not just a brief flurry of activity, but the reorientation of one's entire life.

A true vision always results in concerted action. The late Dr. Martin Luther King, Jr. demonstrated this in a most poignant way with his now famous words, "*I have a dream,*" which will be forever etched on the American conscience. Those otherwise innocuous words took on great meaning when he spoke them, a meaning powerful enough to lay hold of us because they had first powerfully laid hold of him, impelling him to make a total investment of his entire life.

Isaiah cried, "I saw the Lord . . . Here am I. Send me." Dr. King cried, "I just want to do God's will. And He's allowed me to go up to the mountain. . . . And I've seen the promised land. . . . Mine eyes have seen the glory of the coming of the Lord." Both had been laid hold of by a vision. Both lives were revitalized by the vision. It is not necessary to listen to their words to know that. Their actions tell it all!

Actually, a congregation can receive new vitality from either of two sources: a vision or a calamity. Many nearly "dead" congregations have found new vitality through such calamity as the complete destruction of its church building by fire or flood. We hope your congregation may discover new vitality through a vision of its wonderful Lord and its marvelous opportunities to serve Him right where you are.

If this is to happen, however, nothing short of a vision will do. Wishes and dreams are not enough. It will take more than the pastor's routinely saying, "Let's all remember to pray for a revival this week," or the people's dreaming about "the wonderful services we had last year." Revitalization requires a reorientation of the congregation's entire life, an investment of their emotions, energies, time, and money in response to a great and noble purpose that burns in their very souls!

When your people have no vision you can hardly move them to do anything. They might wish a lot, even dream a lot, but do little. But when your people are given a vision, you can hardly stop them from doing everything, giving everything to turn their vision into reality.

Unfortunately, few congregations ever find such a noble, all encompassing purpose that the people willingly, joyfully give all of themselves to it simply because they cannot do otherwise; simply because they have been gifted with a vision, not just any vision, but their very own vision, and now they can really never return to "church as usual" again. They can only say, "Before we only knew what You wanted us to be and do through the words of others (the preacher, Sunday school teachers), but now we have seen You with our own eyes and heard You with our own ears. We have finally climbed our own mountain and beheld the promises of what we, ourselves, can do for You. And now, Lord, we are finally, fully Yours. Here we are. Send us!"

WHERE DO VISIONS COME FROM?

Wishes may be made upon such remote entities as stars, dreams come from within and are attached to our emotions, but visions come from a source outside of and larger than ourselves. They come from the One who is able to offer us a promised land, and to deliver on His promise. Only God can give your people a vision.

Does this mean, then, that we are helpless, that we must stand idly by until the Spirit moves upon the congregation? Not at all! Actually, the pastor can do a great deal, working with the Spirit to prepare the people's hearts and to provide the experiences through which God may sow the seeds of vision. A vision is given to the congregation by God, but the pastor can do much to enable that to happen.

HOW GOD SPEAKS TO THE CONGREGATION

There are three primary ways God speaks to the congregation. He speaks to them individually as they pray and ponder His Word; He speaks to them through the words and lives of others—members, preachers, and teachers; and He speaks to them collectively as they worship, plan, and work together. We will in this book focus our attention on the kind and quality of planning and working together that opens the congregation to God's will, thus allowing Him to give the people a new vision of the church.

Why Planning Is Important

Planning is more important in churches today than it has ever been before. There are several reasons for that. We will discuss two of those: a new type of laity and a turbulent environment.

THE "NEW BREED" OF LAITY

Lay persons in evangelical churches today are better educated and more independent than ever before. With greater education, many are entering professions and assuming positions of greater responsibility. On the job, in the community, and in politics they are thinking for themselves and making greater decisions. A powerful example of this was the active, influential involvement of evangelical Christians in the 1980 national elections. Such political activism on the part of evangelicals was heretofore unthought of, yet in that election they were suddenly highly active in making and breaking the political careers of national leaders and in setting national policy. Evangelical Christians have come to expect such involvement as a right and are now carrying that same expectation into their churches. Today more than ever before they expect to be actively involved in planning the programs and future directions of their church.

In past generations a less educated and more passive laity relied upon the pastor to determine the church's mission and programs for them. Similar behavior on the part of pastors today, however, is being increasingly rejected as authoritarian and unacceptable by a more active and independent laity.

We encounter many pastors in our classes and consultations who bemoan this current state of affairs and wish for a more passive, dependent congregation. We recently heard one troubled pastor exclaim, "I want to keep my lay people ignorant and passive. They cause me less trouble that way!"

A TURBULENT ENVIRONMENT

The environment of every church in America today can best be described as turbulent. Gone (perhaps forever) are the quiet, pastoral days when environmental changes came slowly and predictably. In their place has come an environment characterized by rapid and radical change, an environment that is often indifferent and hostile toward the church. In such an environment a church that fails to do careful planning runs the risk of becoming an island of irrelevancy and ineffectiveness in a hostile sea of need.

Someone recently said, "The future is happening faster than ever before." Actually, in a day of rapid change, the church does encounter the future more quickly than ever before, and with more serious consequence, whether good or bad. For you, therefore, the question is, Who will determine the future of your church? Will it simply react to the forces of indifferent change or will it remain faithful to its vision and prove capable of bringing about some changes on its own? Planning will make the difference.

In *Let My People Go: Empowering Laity for Ministry*, Lindgren and Shawchuck state:

> Planning is like navigation. If you know where you are and where you want to go, navigation is not so difficult. It's when you don't know the two points that navigating the right course becomes difficult. To illustrate this logic, let's use a comparison. Assume you board a luxury ocean liner, its engines already running in preparation to leave port. You go into the chartroom and ask the captain to show you on his charts your present location, what his next port-of-call will be, your final destination; and the route he is planning to get there, and he answers, "I really don't know any of that, I just pay attention to keeping the ship moving." Would you be confident of his reaching his

destination? Would you want to be a passenger on his ship?

Should you not use the same intelligence in planning the future course of your church as you would reasonably expect of the captain? There has never been a church that planned to fail, but there have been many who failed to plan. Unfortunately the results are about the same.[1]

Navigation requires that three points be kept in mind: Where you are now, where you want to go, and the route you will take to get there. Those points are necessary whether you are navigating a ship or a church and can be diagrammed to illustrate a planning process:

THE PLANNING CYCLE

The planning cycle outlined above can open a congregation's eyes to possibilities in ministry that it never saw before. That planning process can lead people up the mountain from which God can show them a promised land of greater effectiveness in service than they ever knew before.

Each of the steps in the planning cycle open up new areas of information and provide the congregation new ways of looking at and thinking about their church and community. In the process new dreams are born and visions are given about what your church can and should be doing to serve God in your community.

MISSION CLARIFICATION (What is God calling us to be and do?)

Mission clarification is the congregation's doing its theological homework.

Mission clarification is not meant to determine specific programs or activities, but to ask the *why* of all activities engaged in and all programs carried on. Goal setting tells "What and How;" mission clarification asks "Why?"

The Lord once said to Jeremiah, "If you extract the precious from the worthless, you will become My spokesman" (Jer. 15:19). A clear, focused understanding of its mission enables a congregation to sort out the precious from the worthless, to focus on the ministries that will turn their visions into realities. Few congregations ever achieve that focus. Instead they go along doing what they have always done, knowing their visions are somehow not being realized and yet not knowing how to focus all of their spiritual, financial, and human resources toward a clearly defined, action-motivating mission. Unfortunately, many pastors seek to escape their own responsibility to lead their congregations in mission clarification and action planning by criticizing those pastors who are most notably successful in doing so.

A clear understanding of a church's mission requires that the people find the relationship among four distinct issues:[2]
1. What do Scripture and our own denominational tradition tell us about our mission?
2. What unique and specific needs and interests do our own members look to our church to fulfill?
3. What specific needs in our community *can* and *should* our church do something about?
4. What specific needs in society and the world *can* and *should* our church do something about?

Occasionally it is very helpful for the congregation to engage in a structured discussion of those four concerns, finally formulating a "mission statement" that sets forth the congregation's understanding of its mission.³

It is in finding the interrelationship among those four concerns that a church comes to understand its mission; that to which God is calling it to *be* and to *do* at this particular time in its particular place. Unfortunately, many evangelicals tend to reject those four components, saying that Scripture alone informs the church of its mission. This is not in keeping with the teachings of Christ, who consistently urged His followers to take a good hard look at the needs of the world around them when determining their mission: "But I say to you, lift up your eyes, and *look on the fields* . . ." (John 4:35, italics added). He sets the conditions of final judgment to include a review of the extent to which they actually respond to those needs (Matt. 25:31-46).

That is what Christ expects from you and your church. Certainly He expects you to look into Scripture for information regarding the mission of your church, but He also expects you to look at your congregation, community, and world for additional, equally important information. The church that fails to do this will someday be called upon to tell why.

Christ is not asking anything of you that He did not do Himself. A careful reading of the gospels clearly shows He looked both to Scripture and at the specific needs of the people and communities to whom He ministered in order to clarify for Himself the mission to which His Father had sent Him (see Matthew 9:36; 14:14; Mark 1:41; 6:34; 8:2-3; Luke 4:17-21). It is important to see in those references that Jesus always tailored His ministry to the needs the people had. To the hungry He gave food, to the sick He gave healing. He could not do otherwise, for He looked so intently at the people and communities around Him that Scripture declares the sight of the people moved (driven as by a storm) Him with compassion for them (Matt. 9:36).

Scripture outlines the *what* and *who* of mission in general terms. The needs of your members and community identify the *what* and *who* of mission in specific, concrete realities.⁴ The following diagram illustrates the relationship of those missional components:⁵

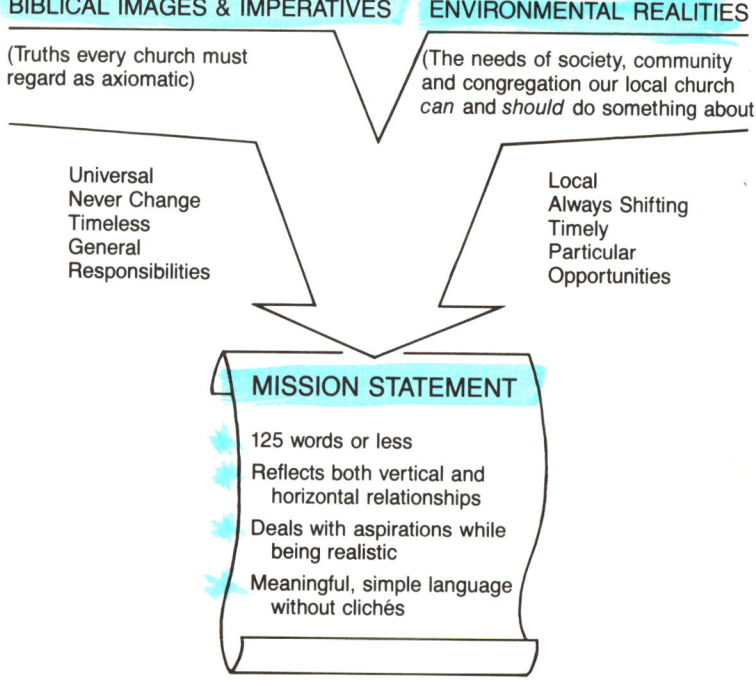

In an excellent book describing his theology of the local church, Jerry Cook says church leaders who look only at Scripture for an understanding of mission tend to see the church as *the field of ministry,* whereas those who also prayerfully seek to respond to concrete needs in the community tend to see the church as *a force for ministry.*[6]

We began this discussion of mission clarification by saying it was the congregation's doing its theological homework. Most people think theology is thinking about and understanding God. Krister Standahl says theology is not thinking about, but thinking about things in a special way. He says, "To do theology is to try to see things as God sees them. The task is so obviously arrogant and oversized that we can only do it playfully, as children. But to children play is serious and creative, and it does something to their growth."[7]

A good place to begin planning in your church is to engage the entire congregation in seriously, creatively, trying to see the needs and opportunities all around you as God might see them. And from that move on to set clear and realistic goals for meeting those needs as God might want them to be met. That is what ministry is all about.

Mission clarification deals with the question of *purpose* in the light of concrete environmental realities. As such it is an ongoing theological activity involving preaching, teaching, and group discussion. It should, however, also be a distinct, intentional step in the planning cycle whenever the congregation is seriously studying its future programs and activities.

In another book, Dr. Perry stresses the importance of a church focusing on clear, specific purposes to revitalization. He says, "Purposes and goals are the key variables in revitalizing a church. When we are dealing with these we are dealing with power! You do not find meaning in a purposeless organization."[8]

CONGREGATIONAL ASSESSMENT (Where are we now?)[9]

There is perhaps no other single activity you can do in your church that has greater potential for generating energy for action than has congregational assessment. That is the testimony we hear from pastors across the country who have taken the bold step to lead their congregation into the planning cycle.

Congregational Assessment Defined. Congregational assessment involves getting members of the congregation together in small groups (7-10 persons) to discuss three questions:

1. What are the strengths of our church? What's going on around here that we feel good about?
2. What are the weaknesses of our church? What's going on around here that we don't feel good about?
3. What are our hopes and dreams for our church over the next one to five years? What suggestions could we make for improving our church?

The information from all the small groups is then compiled under categories (perhaps five to nine), and a brief descriptive paragraph is written for each category. That material, along with the mission statement, becomes the basis for goal setting and planning.

The wisdom of conducting an assessment before making any substantial decisions was clearly taught by our Lord. It is safe to say that it was He who first introduced assessment to the Christian church. In Luke 14:28-31 He talks of sitting down to calculate one's resources before beginning to build a building and of a king's sitting down to take counsel before launching into battle. Congregational assessment is the congregation's sitting down to take counsel regarding its own strengths, weaknesses, hopes, and dreams; and upon the basis of its counsel deciding what its strategy for ministry should be.

An Example of Carrying Out a Congregational Assessment. To help you grasp the assessment process, we share with you actual information given to us by Pastor James McNeill of a congregational assessment conducted by Bethel Evangelical Free Church, North Platte, Nebraska, in 1980. Jim's congregation conducted the assessment by having the small groups meet in fifteen homes. One hundred nineteen members attended the home meetings. The following material is taken directly from Pastor McNeill's notes.

I. CHURCH COUNCIL APPROVAL OF PROJECT
   At the regular monthly church council meeting, May 6, I presented the proposed Congregational Self-Assessment Home Meetings with the following dates for the calendar:
   Monday, June 7, Training Session
   Sunday, June 22, Home Meetings
   Tuesday, June 24, Compiling the Information
   The church council passed a motion approving the project and placing the dates on the calendar.

II. RECRUITMENT OF HOME MEETING LEADERS
   I selected a number of homes from our church directory as potentials for hosting home meetings. I then visited the people in those homes to request they host and lead the home meetings. Fifteen homes quickly volunteered to do so.

III. HOME MEETING TRAINING SESSION, MONDAY, JUNE 9
   In preparation for this session, I reproduced "Outline For Home Meetings #1"[10] and secured newsprint and magic markers.[11] I must admit that I approached this session

thinking that I would have to "sell" these individuals on the concept of self-assessment, home meetings, and their participation as home meeting hosts and hostesses.

As we began, I explained that I would guide them through a "home meeting" format similar to what we would expect them to follow on Sunday, June 22. With the introduction of the first question, "What are the strengths of our church?" two separate groups took newsprint and magic markers with ten minutes allotted to answer the question.

Upon their return, their newsprint was taped to the wall and they reported their responses. The second and third questions were approached in similar fashion. Frankly, following their reporting on the third session, I did not have to do a "sell" job. They were so excited about the process that they were eager to learn and implement a home meeting. My fears had been unfounded. They had caught the value of home meetings.

We reviewed the home meeting outline and discussed:
1. Length of time for answering each of the three questions—consensus came to a thirty-minute time limit.
2. Refreshments—Each host and hostess would serve a light refreshment. A potluck dinner was overruled as potentially asking for too long a block of time from some participants.
3. Time of meeting—General consensus was for 7:00 PM on Sunday, June 22, with some exceptions. Dennis and Cathy Collins preferred Saturday, June 21, for their home meeting and Bud and Ella Brickner would host our older "XYZ" group at a picnic already scheduled for Saturday, June 14.
4. Children—Junior high and high school children would be asked to participate. Each host and hostess would decide whether to suggest a group babysitter or have parents obtain their own babysitters.

We then asked each of them to go through the church directory and select ten to fourteen persons they would like to invite to their home meetings. A sense of excitement continued as the home leaders realized that they would be inviting a core group of persons with whom they had natural friendships, etc. We then reviewed their choices to be sure every church member would be invited to only one home meeting.

IV. THE HOME MEETINGS

The hosts and hostesses personally invited the persons to their home meeting. Total attendance was 119 adults who recorded over four hundred statements to the three questions.

Excitement was expressed by many who attended home meetings. Excellent fellowship and good interaction seemed to be keys to their home meeting excitement.

V. CATEGORIZING THE STATEMENTS

Early on the day following the home meetings the leaders each brought the newsprint of the statements their group had made to the three questions. Dave Johnson, our associate pastor, and I then spent from 8:20 A.M. to 5:10 P.M. with a lunch break, dividing the statements into nine categories. It was exhausting yet exhilarating as we worked through the four hundred statements. Our excitement centered on the fact that the congregation was affirming our areas of strength and also shared the vision of working on specific areas of weaknesses.

We then wrote one sample of a directional statement to be used as a model by all the home meeting leaders when they were to gather the next night to actually write the directional statements for each category.

The next day our secretary typed and mimeographed copies of the categories, each with their related strengths, weaknesses, and hopes and dreams. She also mimeographed our sample directional statement.

VI. "HOME MEETINGS" FOLLOW-UP SESSION WITH THE HOME LEADERS

In preparation for our Tuesday, June 24 session, we taped all the newsprint on the walls of Fellowship Hall in three sections of strengths, weaknesses, and hopes and dreams. As the home leaders arrived, they were instantly attracted to the newsprint to see what other groups had recorded. From 7:00 P.M. to 7:30 P.M. we had them become acquainted with those statements and served iced tea. A lot of interaction began as comments surfaced regarding similarities and uniqueness of statements.

At 7:30 we had the group gather around a circle of chairs in the Fellowship Hall. I asked them for brief statements of their feelings regarding the home meetings. All comments were positive. I then explained that David and I had categorized the statements from their home meetings under nine categories as follows:
1. Staff
2. Lay leadership
3. Christian education
4. Worship
5. Missions
6. Fellowship
7. Finance
8. Facilities
9. Congregation programs

We then distributed the mimeographed copies of the categories and the sample directional statement. I explained that our task for the next several minutes would be to write a directional statement for each category and that each person could pick one of the nine categories, and work with others who would also choose that category to write their directional statements.

At 7:45 P.M. I sent them to various rooms with some newsprint to return at 8:30 P.M. with a completed directional statement. As I moved from group to group, I found two actions surfacing. One was the desire to solve weaknesses, and the other was to get trapped agreeing or disagreeing with one statement of strength or weakness. I reminded the groups of their task and frankly was apprehensive of the possible results to be returned at 8:30.

As the groups regathered at 8:30, I was pleasantly surprised with the quality of statements written. Lay persons have more capabilities than I had imagined! The entire group was excited to hear the statements of the other groups. There was general consensus that we had done a good job.

As we closed, I explained that we would seek to have the results available to the congregation by Sunday, July 6.

VII. DISTRIBUTION OF THE HOME MEETING REPORT

Our volunteer secretaries then typed and mimeographed 150 copies of the categories and directional statements.[12]

We distributed the reports to the congregation on Sunday, June 29, just one week after the home meetings.

The interest in the report was overwhelming. Of the 150 copies, 140 were picked up the first Sunday. Subsequently Patsy Yocum prepared an additional 50 copies for distribution Sunday, July 6.

USING THE ASSESSMENT MATERIAL FOR GOAL SETTING AND PLANNING

After the congregation had an opportunity to review and respond to the assessment material, each category, with its directional statement, was assigned to an appropriate committee for setting congregational goals and plans for (1) capitalizing on the strengths, (2) reducing the weaknesses, and (3) realizing the hopes and dreams of the congregation.

The congregation later approved those goals and plans and committed itself to carry them out.

ADDITIONAL REFLECTIONS ON CONGREGATIONAL ASSESSMENT

The assessment process enables even the most timid lay persons to voice their opinions and dreams regarding the church. Very few lay people have ever done this in such a nonthreatening setting. The pastor is encouraged to attend only one assessment meeting, thus enabling the laity to speak freely among themselves, while at the same time providing a structure whereby all their comments can be collected and reported to the entire congregation.

Some pastors and lay leaders assume they know best the directions the church should take and, therefore, are not too interested in what the laity may be thinking and feeling. Such assumptions on the part of the leaders are a mistake. When it comes to revitalizing a local church one principle that must guide the way decisions are made and programs are carried out is, "People tend to support what they have helped to create." The leaders may have brilliant insight into the church's problems and opportunities, but that will come to little unless the congregation supports their decisions and follows their leading. That will happen when the people themselves are consulted, listened to, and involved in the decision making. Congregational assessment that leads to goal setting leads to action in a powerful and effective way.

The two stages of the planning cycle we have discussed so far constitute the "information gathering" phase of the planning process. What remains now is for the congregation to decide how it will respond to the opportunities, how it will turn its visions into reality. We will discuss the goal setting and implementation phases, in chapter 20.

Notes

1. Alvin J. Lindgrin and Norman Shawchuck, *Let My People Go: Empowering Laity for Ministry* (Nashville: Abingdon, 1980), p. 81.
2. For a further discussion of mission clarification and suggestions as to how a congregation may actually carry out a mission clarification process, see two books by Lindgren and Shawchuck; *Let My People Go* and *Management for Your Church* (Nashville: Abingdon, 1977).
3. For help in leading a congregation through a process of developing a mission statement, see Lindgren and Shawchuck, *Management for Your Church: How to Realize Your Church Potential Through Systems Approach*.
4. One characteristic that generally differentiates "conservative" and "liberal" churches is that the conservatives tend to look only to the Scriptures to identify their mission, whereas the liberals tend to look only to the social and political needs of the community and world. Both views are inadequate to a full understanding of the church's mission.
5. Illustration by Pastor Douglas McIntosh, Stone Mountain Community Church, Tucker, Georgia.

6. Jerry Cook, *Love, Acceptance and Forgiveness* (Glendale, Calif.: Gospel Light, Regal, 1979).
7. Krister Standahl, Dean, Harvard Divinity School, in a lecture in Shalom Center, Sioux Falls, South Dakota, 1979.
8. Lloyd M. Perry, *Getting the Church on Target* (Chicago: Moody, 1977), p. 31.
9. For additional information on congregational assessment, including designs and resources, see Lindgren and Shawchuck, *Let My People Go,* and Robert Worley, *Dry Bones Breathe* (Chicago: Center for the Study of Church Organizational Behavior, 1978).
10. For a copy of the outline Jim used to train the leaders, which they subsequently used to actually lead the meetings, see Appendix A.
11. Newsprint is the large sheets of paper used to print newspapers. You can purchase it from office supply stores or print shops.
12. For an actual sample of one of the categories along with its responses and directional statements, see Appendix B.

2

Planning to Make Your Visions Come True: Goal Setting, Implementation and Evaluation

For want of skilful strategy
 an army is lost;
Victory is the fruit of long
 planning.
Prov. 11:14, NEB*

Said Alice to the cheshire cat:
 "Would you tell me, please, which way I ought to go from here?"
Said the cat:
 "That depends a good deal on where you want to get to."
 "I don't much care where. . . ," said Alice.
 "Then," said the cat, "it doesn't matter which way you go."

A congregation that has completed a mission clarification and an assessment process is certainly much more fortunate than Alice was when she met the cat. That congregation has a vision of where it wants to go. What remains now is for it to plan specific ways to get there. The planning cycle allows the people to do that in two states: first, specific goals (targets) are set; then concrete implementation strategies are planned to accomplish the goals. That is the goal setting and implementation phase of the planning cycle, as it is outlined below.

GOAL SETTING (Where do we want to be?)

In the preceding chapter we suggested that the entire congregation be urged to participate in developing the mission

---
New English Bible.

statement and the congregational assessment. That information, generated by the congregation, can now be used by the ruling board, program committees, or a special planning committee to establish goals and to do the planning to carry out those goals.

Goal setting based upon the congregation's assessment and mission statement results in a "how to" plan for the church, a plan that guides the church in going from where it is to where it wants to be at some point in the future.

The mission statement and the assessment directional statements point the directions. The goals state what the church will do to move in those directions and establish clearly defined targets at which the congregation can aim; targets of which the congregation can say, "When we achieve these targets we will have reduced our weaknesses, accomplished some of our hopes and dreams, and come closer to fulfilling our mission."

Goals, therefore, are *means* to move the congregation in the directions it wants to go. They are not *ends* in themselves, but means to help the congregation accomplish the end results; its mission.[1]

The goal is a description of a desired future condition the group wants to achieve. For the congregation to know whether it ever achieves its aim, goals need to be stated in specific, concrete terms and in such a way that they can somehow be measured—numbers, time-line, percentages, certain conditions.

Measurability is an important concept in writing goals. There is a great danger, however, that as the group writes its goals in measurable terms the goals may become mathematical statements; a 10 percent increase in Sunday school attendance, fifteen more people in prayer meetings, an increase in contributions of $50.00 per week. Some church goals perhaps should be quantitative. But the church is a qualitative institution, and the majority of its goals should be statements of desired qualities, not quantities. They should describe ministries that capture the hearts and minds of the people, not mathematical problems that send them scrambling for their pocket calculators.[2]

Other terms are also used to describe what we are here referring to as a "goal." Some of those terms are; *target, objective, plan.* The terms you use are not important so long as you understand how all of the steps fit together to make a complete, progressive planning process. To help people understand how we use the terms and how they fit together, we sometimes use the following illustration to show how ideas are funneled through the process to result in concrete plans.

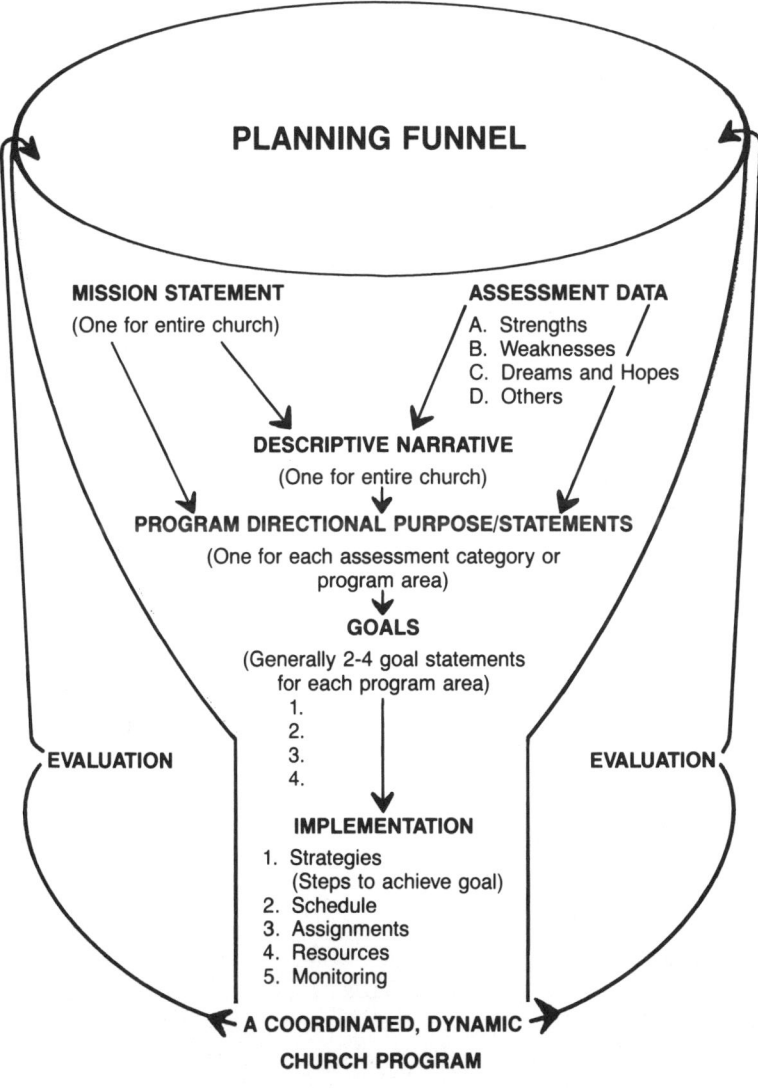

To further assist groups to write qualitative goals that are also measurable, we suggest the following Guidelines for Writing Goals.

A goal should meet as many as possible of the following tests:

1. *It is mission-directed*: It can be clearly seen as a help toward achieving the church's mission.

2. *It is desirable*: It grows out of congregational interests and needs which have been expressed, or represents conviction about its need for a more healthy and effective church organization.

3. *It is conceivable*: It can be expressed in clearly understandable words.

4. *It is assignable*: Persons asked to achieve it can see their tasks clearly.

5. *It is believable*: Its accomplishment can be visualized as entirely possible.

6. *It is achievable*: The existing resources (or those that can be secured) of time, skills, materials, facilities, persons, and dollars are sufficient to do the task.

7. *It is measurable*: It is possible to tell when it has been accomplished, and some judgment can be made as to whether it was worthwhile to do.

8. *It is controllable*: It produces a minimum of unintended consequences; persons and groups are not involved unintentionally or without their permission.[3]

In order to assist groups to meet those guidelines we have developed a planning worksheet. By preparing a worksheet for the goal, you will not only have succeeded in building in a degree of measurability, but will also have determined the implementation procedures for carrying out the goal.

Use of the worksheet causes the group to consider certain key issues that determine how the goal will be implemented; how it will be carried out.

IMPLEMENTATION (How do we plan to get there?)

A goal well planned is 50 percent achieved. Every year hundreds of churches write thousands of goals that are never carried out. This is due by and large to the fact that the guidelines

PLANNING WORKSHEET

Goal: (Write in measurable terms, if possible.)

Date: _____
Goal Manager: _____
Check-Up Dates: _____

What Steps Will We Take To Achieve the Goal?	Who Will Be Responsible For This Step?	When Is It To Be Done?	What Resources Will Be Needed?	What Will The Result/Product Be?

for writing goals are not adhered to and that good implementation plans are not made.

In *Let My People Go: Empowering Laity for Ministry*, Lindgren and Shawchuck describe the components of a good implementation plan. They say:

> Good implementation begins with developing a good plan. This plan needs to be written and comprehensive enough to serve as a "road map" to achieving the goals. A road map that is so incomplete as to leave out important information is no good, and one that is cluttered with unimportant and confusing material is also no good. A good implementation plan will give information regarding the following:
>
> Strategizing: *What* activities will we do to reach our goal?
>
> Scheduling: *When* will each activity take place?
>
> Recruiting and Assigning: *Who* is responsible to see that it happens?
>
> Resourcing: *What* are the equipment, space, money and worker needs to carry out the activity?
>
> Monitoring: *How* will we check up to be sure the plan is functioning properly and on time?

Strategizing:

A good place to begin in developing action plans is to choose your "route"; the steps or activities to achieve the goal. Remember, just like a road map, there are always many "routes" you can follow to reach your destination; your goal. And each route may have many steps along the way. The routes you follow should be carefully selected, based upon people's interests, abilities, available resources.

You may choose to brainstorm many activities and then select those which seem most feasible. After you have decided upon the activities the next step is to put them into sequential order, thus providing a list of activities and the order in which they will be carried out in order to reach the goal.

Scheduling:

After the activities are chosen and put into sequential order, a calendar is developed showing when each activity is to be completed. If the list of activities is very long or complex, this can sometimes be a difficult task. A helpful technique is to first establish the beginning and ending points; the date activities are to begin on the goal, and the date when all activities are to be completed. Having established these two points, continue scheduling from the beginning point until reaching the point where you are no longer sure of dates, time needed to do a step, etc. Then begin scheduling from the ending point back toward the front. Continue this until reaching a point of uncertainty. With this new information schedule move some more from the front, then again from the back, etc. until both schedules are met in the middle.

Recruiting and Assigning:

Having built the schedule, the next step is to recruit someone for each step to be responsible to see that the step is carried out on time. Many church planning processes go awry at the points of scheduling and recruiting/assigning. They fail to clearly schedule each step and/or they fail to assign persons to be specifically responsible to carry out each step.

Following are some rules which, if adhered to, should enhance your implementation efforts:

1. Assign no one to any task until they have been personally contacted and have freely volunteered to do the task.

To assign anyone to a task without first getting their consent is a sure road to frustration and failure. Such action often results in noncommited workers who fail to carry out their responsiblities. If you should ever remind them of their responsibilities, they cry, "Hey, what do you expect of me? I never wanted this job in the first place!"

If any goal cannot readily generate sufficient volunteer interest to carry it out, it is safe to assume it will never be carried out and should be abandoned. This process is one means of deciding which goals are in fact priorities for the people.

   2. Each step is assigned to someone who has agreed to be responsible to see that the step is carried out on schedule.

That person is not necessarily responsible to do the work, but to see that it is done. He/she may likely have to recruit others to work with him/her.

A common tendency (pit-fall) for church planning groups is to expect that the entire committee will assume responsibility to see that all the steps are carried out. This is courting failure! When everyone is responsible no one is accountable, and "Let George do it" reigns supreme.

Resourcing:

Asking someone to take a position, or to do some activity in the church, carries with it the moral responsibility to provide that person with the necessary resources to do the job well. Resourcing, therefore, becomes an important part of implementation planning. It does little good to plan a program if you will not have the resources to carry it out.

Resourcing involves determining and providing for such needs as equipment, space, money, volunteer workers. Resourcing needs for simple programs can be quickly identified. More complex programs, however, may require careful analysis and resource planning.

Monitoring:

This involves determining how the entire plan will be followed to be sure it functions properly and on time. The earlier implementation steps of strategizing, scheduling, and assigning provide the framework for monitoring. Monitoring questions are:

   1. Where are we in the plan, what steps are accomplished, and what should we do next?
   2. Are the steps being done according to schedule? If not, what adjustments should be made to get the plan back on schedule?
   3. Are the workers doing their job satisfactorily? Are

they in need of resources? Do we need additional workers?

We suggest two principles to assure the monitoring function is carried out in such a way as to help the program on target:

1. When preparing the implementation strategy, schedule check-up dates at crucial points to review the progress and results of the plan.
2. Appoint a "goal monitor" whose responsibility is to monitor the entire plan. The goal monitor is responsible to remind persons of their assignments far enough in advance to ensure they have not forgotten. The goal monitor also stays in close touch with workers, providing resources, helping to solve problems and to spot any potential breakdown of the plan before it happens. If the goal monitor cannot solve the problem, he/she will request help from the pastor, administrative board, etc.[4]

Use of the planning worksheet, will ensure that all of these critical implementation issues will be cared for before the group begins work on actually carrying out the goal. It is this type of planning that ensures the congregation will succeed in moving from where it is to where it wants to be.

EVALUATION (How close did we come to our destination?)

Evaluation is the missing link in most church planning activities. The fact that most church leaders do not evaluate their efforts is due not so much to a lack of skill as it is due to a lack of nerve. Many church leaders do not want to know how well, or how poorly, they are doing. Many are plagued with a feeling of ineffectiveness, and they fear evaluation will only serve to make public and obvious what they are already thinking and feeling in secret about the results of their work.

In addition, pastors often tell us they are reluctant to evaluate lay workers, because "after all, they are volunteering their time." This attitude, however, often has a reverse effect of causing the lay workers to feel that whatever it is they are doing is really not very important because no one seems to care whether they are doing a good or a poor job.

AN EVALUATION PROCESS

Following is a list of questions we find helpful in guiding church groups regarding the kinds of information they need to do good evaluation.[5]

I. Evaluation of Goals and Objectives
   A. What are the goals we have been pursuing?
   B. Are these goals coherent with our mission? Are they the right goals?
   C. Are the goals clear (do we know what we have to do to achieve them?) and realistic (can we hope to achieve them?)?
II. Evaluation of Programs and Activities
   A. Is our program(s) coherent with our mission and goals?
   B. To what extent is our program(s) achieving its goals? Is it effective?
   C. Is our program(s) worth the time, effort, and money we are putting into it? Is it efficient?
   D. Are there any positive and/or negative side effects? Are our programs causing any unplanned, unanticipated results?
III. Problem Solving and Future Planning
   A. What changes need to be made in our present program(s) to make it more effective in reaching our goals and mission?
   B. What new goals and programs do we need to help us achieve our mission?

Evaluation that results in answers to those questions serves two important purposes: it helps monitor existing programs to identify needed changes while there is still time for the changes to make a difference, and it identifies new programs and activities that may be needed to help the church accomplish its mission.

Evaluation should be going on throughout the entire planning process and should be conducted in such a way as to allow all the members to offer evaluation, not just pastors and lay officers.

Most church groups conducting evaluation do so by means of a questionnaire survey. Our experience is that that is perhaps the poorest method. People do not generally like to fill out questionnaires, having been conditioned to them in unpleasant situations; filling out income tax forms, standing in long lines during college registration, in order to get into a hospital when ill. It is not too surprising to discover patient and pleasant church members responding with disinterest or hostility when confronted with questionnaires from the church.

A generally better approach is to use evaluation methods that enable persons to communicate together in face-to-face settings regarding their opinions of the church program. Such methods as small group discussion, personal interviews, public hearings, or telephone interviews may be considered. When using those methods a questionnaire may sometimes be effective to facilitate and focus discussion so that the desired information is generated.

Finally, evaluation should be as much a "style" as it is a distinct activity. Distinct times and processes by which the church evaluates the effectiveness of its programs are important. Equally important, however, is to develop a norm in which it is all right for the congregation to ask how well its programs are doing and to give and receive honest feedback all along the way, not just at certain times of the year when the church evaluates its programs.

Conclusion: Planning to Make Your Visions Come True

In the book *Strategy for Leadership* the authors state that goals will have more of an impact on the future of your organization than anything else.

It is obvious that any book on church revitalization must include the planning process as a major ingredient. Perhaps no other single method can involve so many members in such significant ways. The laity experience this type of involvement as revitalizing. This results in an increased commitment on their part to help support and carry out the programs that have been planned.

Speaking in favor of the kind of planning process we have described, Dr. Thomas Gordon states:

> No one is apathetic except in pursuit of someone else's goals. . . . People work hard to accomplish goals they set

for themselves. But they experience this opportunity so rarely that you can expect a burst of enthusiasm when they are given the chance. People get sick of having someone else set goals for them, not because they resent authority, but because they have talent that is not being used. They want to exercise their [own] muscles. . . . People are happier when given a chance to accomplish more. A sense of accomplishment, the feeling that they have done something worthwhile, brings most people pleasure and a sense of importance. The more often they can experience these satisfying feelings, the more interested and enthusiastic they will become and the more they will attempt to repeat the experience. The challenge to you as a [pastor] is to see how often you can give [them] such opportunities.[6]

Goal setting is important only for churches who want to get somewhere, who want to succeed in their ministry. For all other churches, it is a waste of time and effort.

The major intent of the planning process is to give the congregation a clear-cut sense of purpose for ministry beyond the elementary aspects of repentance. That sense of purpose will give the congregation vision and power. In his famous new book *Leadership* Burns says: "There is nothing so power-full, nothing so deceptive, nothing so casual as common purpose if that purpose informs all levels of the organization. . . . Moreover, unity of purpose and congruence of motivation fosters casual influence far down the line. Nothing can substitute for common purpose. . . ."[7]

A major complaint we hear from pastors is that goal setting does not allow room for the Holy Spirit to move in the church. That is pure nonsense. Surely the Holy Spirit can influence and direct the thinking and acting of persons who are intentional about ministry as much as he can that of persons who muddle along with no intentions at all.

Paul was very much a goal-directed person, and he was led by the Holy Spirit. The Holy Spirit was not hindered by Paul's goals. He was able to speak to Paul precisely because they had specific goals to talk about. A careful reading of Act 16 should be sufficient to convince you of this. According to verse 6, the Spirit told him not to speak in Phrygia and Galatia, though it was his goal to strengthen the churches in that area. According to verse 7, it was Paul's goal to go to Bithynia, but the Spirit said "no" to this goal. According to verse 9, the Spirit then gave Paul a vision and in it a new direction: Macedonia.

It is a quality of visions that they come to people who are goal-minded, not to muddlers who excuse their lack of planning and work by saying they are waiting for the Lord to direct them. You are much better off to move, go in some direction, give God something concrete to talk to you about. You will then discover that God can and does reveal His will in the midst of our best efforts to be intentional about our ministry.

Jesus was goal-minded in all that He did so that He was able to say to Pilate, "For this I have come into the world, to bear witness to the truth" (John 18:37). Paul was goal-minded. The cheshire cat reminded Alice that it would be much easier to give her directions if she had some goal, some direction in mind. We urge you to put away from your thinking once and for all the idea that goal setting hinders the Holy Spirit. Scripture simply does not bear this out.

Perhaps no church leader in this century has done more to revitalize the ministry of lay groups than did Belgium's Bishop Joseph Cardijn. He succeeded in describing the entire planning process in three short words: *see, judge, act*. He said:

> This is the method . . . see, judge, act. . . . A concrete method, realistic and effective.
> See— open your eyes and look around you. Start with life itself. Discover the personal, social, political, religious needs around you.
> Judge—Look at these needs objectively. How does God feel about this? What does He want us to do about it? What can you do about them? How can you do it? When? What resources do you have to do it?
> Act— Strive to transform these needs. Mobilize your resources and take concrete action. Act to make your church, your community and world a better place.

Bishop Cardijn wrote only one book in his lifetime, entitled *Laymen into Action*. In that book he said:

> Laymen are formed first by the discovery of facts, followed

by a Christian judgment, resulting in the actions they plan, the plans they carry into effect, the responsibilities they shoulder.

The challenge is this, how can all men (and women) each one be made aware that they have a mission on earth that God Himself has entrusted to them from the very moment of the creation and the redemption, a mission the church proclaims to them and helps them to realize? What can be done to make each person live with this unshakable conviction: "God needs me! I am His missionary!?"

For me laypersons are not formed for their own ministry through books, purely theoretical teaching, or spoken lectures (sermons), however magnificent, or even through discussions. . . . Laymen are formed first of all by the discovery of facts, followed by a Christian judgment, resulting in actions they plan, the plans they carry into effect, the responsibilities they shoulder.[8]

Cardijn also said we act either individually or as a group. However, the action must be specific. The necessity of material, temporal applications of the Gospel has to be faced. "To the extent that you did it to one these brothers of Mine, even the least of them, you did it to Me" (Matt. 25:40).

In order for the church and its laity to be revitalized each one individually and collectively must be given a vision of the ministry they can perform. They must *see, judge, act*. The planning cycle is a powerful method for allowing that to happen. It can be, therefore, a revitalizing and profoundly religious process that will lead your church closer to the heart and will of Christ for your church. It all needs to be done in the context of much prayer and reflection. That will ensure that the goals and plans reflect the mind of God for your church, and not merely the conglomerate opinion of the people.

All planning processes in the church must be saturated with a great deal of prayer, teaching, and theological reflection at each stage of the planning cycle. Each goal, each new program must be approved not by majority vote, but by the congregation's sensing the Spirit's leading in that direction.

The Spirit cannot lead people unless they are already going somewhere, and He will not direct people who are not already doing something. His coveted words, "This is the way, walk in it" are reserved only for those who are already on the way to somewhere. The planning cycle, therefore, can be a powerful means through which God can break through with the vision that leads to action and vitality. The planning cycle, when prayerfully, faithfully carried out, can become a "vision cycle" for your church.

In *Getting the Church on Target*, Dr. Perry says,

> Clarifying purposes and establishing goals are lost arts in churches, homes and individual lives. Our purposes and goals, conscious or unconscious, largely determine what direction our lives take and whether or not we find freedom and fulfillment as individuals and members of the human family. Clear purposes and goals force people to become specific in their thinking.
>
> Purposes and goals are the key variables in revitalizing the church. When we are dealing with these, we are dealing with power. You do not find meaning in a purposeless organization.[9]

Some years have now passed since Dr. Perry wrote his book. We have had many additional opportunities to test its veracity. We remain fully convinced that a key element of church revitalization is in fact working to get the church on target through a clear sense of purpose and meaningful goals.

In the popular song, Mona Lisa, the beautiful lady is accused of being something of a dream-killer. "Many dreams have been brought to your doorstep, they just lie there and they die there. . . ." Miss Mona is not alone in this, however. Rather, she joins the ranks with hundreds of pastors and lay leadership committees who lead congregations to set goals but who fail to create the organizational structures needed to carry out those goals. To such church leaders the congregation could very well sing, "We have brought our hopes and dreams to your door-step, they just lie there and they die there. . . ." Goal setting is not enough. After the goals are set, they must be supported by appropriate organizational structures. Creating those structures will be the topic of the following chapter.

> Commit your works to the LORD,
> And your plans will be established.
> Proverbs 16:3

NOTES

1. For an excellent discussion on the difference between "means" and "ends" in planning see Roger Kaufman, *Identifying and Solving Problems: A Systems Approach* (San Diego, Calif.: University Associates, 1976).
2. We do not want this discussion to imply that quality cannot be measured! We urge every pastor and church leader to read chapter 12, "Why Service Institutions Do Not Perform," in Peter Drucker, *Management* (New York: Harper & Row, 1973).
3. Adapted from Robert C. Worley, "Congregational Involvement Through a Goal Setting Process," mimeographed (Chicago: Center for the Study of Church Organization Behavior, 1975).
4. Alvin J. Lindgren and Norman Shawchuck, *Let My People Go: Empowering Laity for Ministry* (Nashville: Abingdon, 1980), pp. 84-91.
5. Gustave Rath, Karen Stoyanoff, and Norman Shawchuck, *Fundamentals of Evaluation* (Downers Grove, Ill.: Organization Resources, 1979), pp. 8-10.
6. Thomas Gordon, *Leader Effectiveness Training* (New York: Wyden, 1977), pp. 244-45.
7. James McGregor Burns, *Leadership* (New York: Harper & Row, 1978), p. 439.
8. Joseph Cardijn, *Laymen Into Action* (London: Geoffrey Chapman, 1964), pp. 19, 21, 50.
9. Lloyd M. Perry, *Getting the Church on Target* (Chicago: Moody, 1977), p. 31.

3

Organizing for Action

One of our students is the pastor of a Baptist church with about ninety members. He had just led his congregation through the mission clarification and congregational assessment and was calling to discuss the next step in the revitalization process. The conversation went as follows:

> Hey, prof, we appointed a steering committee to lead our church through the planning cycle and we did the mission clarification process just like you described it in *Management for Your Church*.[1] Gangbusters! The whole congregation got into the act and we came out with a mission statement and everybody asking, "What do we do next?"
>
> Now, we have just completed the congregational assessment. Gangbusters again! We did the home meetings using the outline about as you gave it in class.[2] Just about every member attended a home meeting and there was great discussion about where our church is going. It's like an old fashioned revival around here.
>
> Now what do we do? The steering committee is asking what we do next and I don't know. How do we set goals? Does the whole congregation set goals, or does the steering committee do this?

Our friend was struggling with the issue of how to organize the church for action. The mission statement had been prepared and the assessment completed. Now it was time for action; it was time to organize the church to carry out its mission and to turn its hopes and dreams into reality.

He told us they had organized the assessment data into six categories: pastoral ministry, missions and local outreach, buildings and grounds, regular services and programs, spiritual health and growth, and general internal organization. They had also written a directional statement for each category and a narrative description of the state of the entire church.

He also told us the present organizational structure of the church is composed of four major committees: church advisory board, board of trustees, Christian education committee, and missions committee. In addition, there are a few minor committees, such as music and memorials.

We suggested he prepare a list of assessment categories and of the existing committees as follows:

Existing Committees
1. Advisory Board
2. Board of Trustees
3. Christian Education
4. Missions
5. Music
6. Memorials

Assessment Categories
1. Pastoral Ministry
2. Missions and Local Outreach
3. Buildings and Grounds
4. Special Services & Events
5. Spiritual Growth & Ministry

Then we asked him to review the directional statement for each assessment category to decide which categories would clearly fit into the work areas of existing committees. He decided that two categories clearly fit into the work areas of any existing committees; building and grounds clearly fit into the work of the board of trustees, and "missions" fit with the missions committee, although the "local outreach" was going beyond anything the committee had previously been expected to do. He visited with the missions committee about local outreach. The committee said they did have time to give, and could be expected to add local outreach to their work area.

That left four assessment categories that did not fit into the work area of any existing committee. We decided the Christian education committee already had plenty to do and should not be considered for any additional assignments.

Having made all the assignments that were to be made to

existing committees, we suggested the church appoint a special task force to each be responsible for one of the remaining categories, with the exception of pastoral ministry, which we suggested might become the responsibility of the advisory board.

The present advisory board comprised seven members. We suggested the size of the advisory board be expanded to allow one member to be assigned to each of the existing committees and the new task forces, plus an advisory board chairperson who would not be assigned to another committee.

When that was completed the church had organized itself for action, creating a structure in which one committee was responsible to establish and implement goals for each assessment category and would move the church in the direction the congregation had set for that specific category, all in harmony with the church's mission statement. The following diagram outlines their new organizational structure:

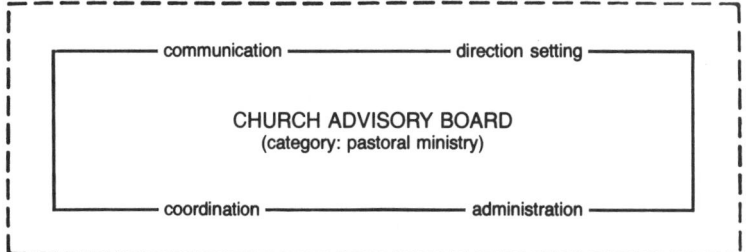

EXISTING (ongoing)
COMMITTEES/BOARDS

1. Missions
   (category: Missions & Local Outreach)
2. Trustees
   (category: Building & Grounds)
3. Christian Education
4. Music Committee
5. Memorials

communication — direction setting

CHURCH ADVISORY BOARD
(category: pastoral ministry)

coordination — administration

SPECIAL TASK FORCES

1. Regular Services & Programs
2. Spiritual Health & Growth
3. General Internal Organizations

In this process each committee or task force should be given as much freedom as possible to creatively set the goals and plan the programs for their work area. At the same time the groups must do that in keeping with the will of the congregation as expressed in the mission statement and congregational assessment.

1. The entire congregation is invited and urged to participate in preparing the mission statement and the congregational assessment.

2. The steering committee and the home meeting leaders develop the action categories, a statement describing the direction the congregation wants to move in each area, and a narrative description of the overall "state of the church."

3. Each ongoing committee or task force to whom an action category is assigned is provided with the mission statement, all the assessment information relative to its action category, the directional statement for that category, and the description of the "state of the church." All of that information is also given to the congregation.

4. The committees and task forces then use the material to set the goals and plan programs for their action category.

5. The goals and plans are presented to the congregation for review and adoption.

6. The committees and task forces then implement their plans.

When the church had completed steps 1 through 5 each group set about to implement its plans. The steering committee had now completed its task and was dissolved so that its members could join other committees.

The enthusiasm and expectation reported in the congregation as it worked its way through the planning cycle and organized itself to accomplish its goals is something that many churches have reported to us. The congregation has discovered a new vision and the motivation to make their vision into reality.

Form Follows Function

In efforts to revitalize the church, planning and organizing are essential twins-in-the-process. Organization and action without visions and plans becomes anarchy. Visions and plans without organization and action become "pipe dreams"; unfulfilled fantasies that pastor and people intend to accomplish—someday.

Form Follows Function is an important principle to remember. Planning answers the function question, "What will we do?" Organizational structure answers the form question, "How will we organize ourselves to do it?"

Unfortunately most churches pay very little attention to tailoring organizational structures to most effectively achieve the goals they are trying to accomplish. The church traditionally attempts to keep the organizational structures unchanged, no matter what the goals or programs may be. That is perhaps due in large part to the pressures brought to bear upon pastors and local churches by denominational officials who often believe all churches must be alike organizationally if they are not to lose their denominational identity. We suggest, however, that a denomination's identity and cohesiveness is sustained by its theology and ecclesiology, and not the shape of its organizational structures on the denominational or local levels.

Form Follows Function implies that planning in your church may very well not be fully effective until you have altered your organizational structures in the light of the new goals and programs you have adopted in the planning process. Jesus spoke of the wisdom of allowing new goals to influence the structures that are intended to carry them when He said, "Nor do men put new wine into old wineskins; otherwise the wineskins burst, and the wine pours out, and the wineskins are ruined; but they put new wine into fresh wineskins, and both are preserved" (Matt. 9:17).

After the congregation has worked through the planning process, do all you can to preserve the new vision and plans by altering existing structures and/or creating new ones to coordinate all the resources of the church to achieve those plans.

ONGOING PROGRAMS AND CHANGE PROGRAMS

There are two types of programs a church may have: ongoing and change. Ongoing programs are those that are often basic to the church's life and functions, composed of the necessary, permanent strategies and committees to carry on routine or administrative programs and tasks; i.e., the Sunday school, the finance committee. Change programs are generally ad hoc or short-term strategies and committees established to accomplish specific, time-bounded change goals; for example, constructing a new Christian education unit, conducting a churchwide goal-setting process.

Most churches put all their attention to maintaining ongoing programs. Their motto is, "What we have done before we will do forever—and nothing more," or "through weal or woe our status is quo." Such behavior, if it continues in any church, in today's situation only spells disaster. The church today lives and works in a context of rapid and radical change; individual members' interests and abilities are changing; communities are changing; social and economic systems are changing. Those many changes require that the local church also change or else become an isolated island of irrelevancy in a sea of tremendous human need and suffering.

There is a delightful poem we often quote to highlight the folly of clinging to old ideas and approaches simply because "that's the way we've always done it." It is titled "Calf Paths of the Mind."

> One day through the primeval wood,
>   a calf walked home as good calves should;
> but made a trail all bent askew,
>   a crooked trail as calves all do.
> Since then, three hundred years have fled,
>   and I infer the calf is dead.
> But still he left behind his trail,
>   and thereby hangs my morale tale.
> The trail was taken up next day
>   by a long dog that passed that way;
> and then a wise bellwether sheep
>   pursued the trail o'er vale and steep
> and drew the flock behind him, too,
>   as good bellwethers always do.
> And from that day, o'er hill and glade;
>   through these old woods a path was made.
> And many men wound in and out,
>   and dodged and turned and bent about.
> And uttered words of righteous wrath

because t'was such a crooked path;
but still they followed . . . do not laugh,
   the first migrations of that calf.
This forest path became a lane,
   that bent and turned and turned again.
This crooked lane became a road,
   where many a poor horse with his load
toiled on beneath the burning sun
   and traveled some three miles in one.
And thus a century and a half
   they trod the footsteps of that calf.
The years passed on in swiftness fleet;
   the road became a village street;
and this, before men were aware,
   a city's crowded thoroughfare.
And soon the central street was this
   of a renowned metropolis.
And men two centuries and a half
   trod in the footsteps of that calf,
a hundred thousand men were led
   by one calf near three centuries dead.
For men are prone to go it blind
   along the calf-paths of the mind
and work away from sun to sun
   to do what other men have done.
They follow in the beaten track
   and out and in, and forth and back,
and still their devious course pursue,
   to keep the path that others do.
They keep the path a sacred groove
   along which all their lives they move.
but how the wise old wood gods laugh
   who saw the first primeval calf![3]

The planning process helps congregations break out of its "old ruts," to determine the changes that are needed in programs, goals, and organizational structures to foster and maintain new levels of ministry effectiveness.

Change, however, must be planned and managed. To cause changes in the church simply for the sake of "having something new" or "getting rid of this because its old" can only lead to trouble. Many of the old programs of the church are still vital. Sunday school has been around a long time and still remains one of the most vital programs in the church.

What the church needs, then, is a balance between ongoing programs to keep the best of what it now has and the change programs needed to continually renew itself. Those are coordinated to accomplish the vision the church has for its life and ministry.

Ongoing programs carry out very different functions from change programs. Ongoing programs are administrative, more or less permanent, and give attention to maintaining long-range programs and activities. Change programs are innovative and come into and go out of existence as needed. Programs for change should never continue beyond the time established to carry out a specific goal, and give attention to creating new programs and activities or to creating change within conditions of an ongoing program. Due to the differences in function and style it is essential that the work of all those units be coordinated by a central coordinating unit such as the administrative board.

To ensure that its organizational structure is kept current with the church's mission and goals for ministry, the entire program structure should be plotted on paper and revised at least annually, according to the church's ongoing and change goals for the year. We have already given you one example of how a church might organize itself for action around the categories it has identified as being the areas in which it wants action. The chart on the next page is an example of an action oriented program structure that utilizes ongoing committees to take care of permanent programs and ad hoc committees to work in areas of change.

How might this type of program structure help to revitalize a church?

1. The ongoing structures ensure that vital, long-range needs are met.

2. The change structures ensure that the church is constantly renewing itself to meet new needs in the congregation and community and new interests in the congregation.

3. The annual review of all programs and needs ensures no programs continue beyond their usefulness and that no needed program areas are overlooked.

Program Structure of Community Church for 1983

ON-GOING PROGRAMS

1. Worship & Music
2. Sunday School
3. Trustee Board
4. Women's Group
5. Finance Committee
6. Youth Group
7. Memorial Committee

These are all permanent committees responsible to administer ongoing programs and functions.

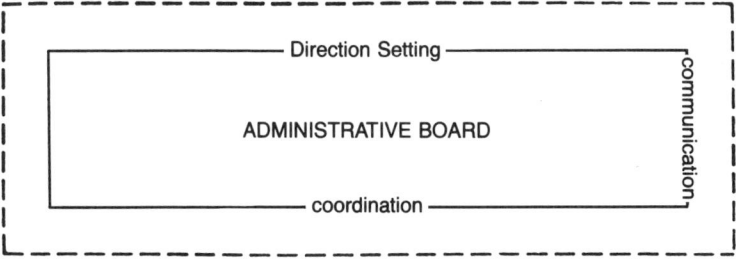

Administrative board composed of one representative from each ongoing and change committee, elected by the committees, plus the chairperson, who is elected by the congregation.

CHANGE PROGRAMS

1. Committee on congregational self-assessment & goal setting.
2. Committee on 1985 guided tour of Holy Land.
3. Committee to secure $40,000 for Christian coffee house.
4. Committee on "All-music" worship services.

These are all ad hoc committees, each responsible for one specific change objective and designed to go out of existence when that objective is met.

4. Short-range change committees open up service opportunities to many more people and allow individuals to volunteer for a particular program based upon the length of time commitment they wish to make. The length of time commitments in the ongoing programs are generally quite long; one to four years; whereas the change programs may require a six-week, six-month, or perhaps one-year commitment.

5. The use of change committees will allow ongoing committees to do a better job. A common mistake made in churches whenever a change goal is set is to give the responsibility for that new program to an already existing ongoing committee. The new assignment is almost always viewed as an unwanted burden upon the committee's already crowded agenda. As a consequence the change goal is never accomplished or accomplished poorly. The committee is disspirited and guilty over not doing their whole job. As a result their ongoing responsibilities are now done with less enthusiasm and effectiveness. The "new wine" poured into the old "wineskin" causes the quality of both to be lost.

Whenever it can be accomplished, a change program should be given to a committee created for that specific purpose. If a change goal is given to an ongoing committee, it should only be because the committee sincerely wants to do it and has the time to give to it without damaging the ongoing program.

The net result of this type of programming is that many more people can be actively involved in the ministry of the church, all programs can be strengthened, and the church can keep responsive to all needs. By doing so they experience a new level of effectiveness and vitality. This is what we mean by revitalization.

Conclusion

In this chapter we have attempted to demonstrate that new goals and programs often, if not always, call for new committees and policies to implement them. In addition, we have said that all of the material generated in the mission clarification and the congregational assessment can be collected into "action categories." Those categories themselves will suggest the number and type of program committees that are needed, both ongoing and ad hoc. We also said the chances for success in each action area are greatly enhanced when an action area becomes the one and only agenda for a committee or task force, so that it is able to give all of its attention to that area.

Having good plans and designing effective structures, however, is not enough. Every plan needs leaders and workers, every structure needs people to breathe life into it. Therefore, an important ingredient in any revitalization process must be the recruitment and development of effective, dedicated people to carry out the plans and programs of the church. The following chapter will take up a discussion of leadership development.

NOTES

1. Alvin J. Lindgrin and Norman Shawchuck, *Management for Your Church: How to Realize Your Church's Potential Through Systems Approach* (Nashville: Abingdon, 1977).
2. This outline is printed in Alvin J. Lindgrin and Norman Shawchuck, *Let My People Go: Empowering Laity for Ministry* (Nashville: Abingdon, 1980), and in Appendix A of this book.
3. Poem supplied by Dr. Don Messer, President, Dakota Wesleyan University, who informs us the author of the poem is unknown.

4

Developing Church Leadership

We have discussed ideas and programs for revitalizing your church: mission clarification, organizational assessment, and goal setting. Each of those, to be at all successful, requires leadership and participation of the laity. The pastor can do none of those alone, and that is the way it should be. A church is revitalized through its members as they, one-by-one, take on new and larger responsibilities that move them from being passive "pew warmers" to active planners and doers of ministry.

The Pastor's Role in Developing Church Leadership

The whole idea of creating a powerful, active laity is met with mixed emotions on the part of clergy, many of whom are not fully willing to accept the laity as genuine co-workers in the church. Many clergy fear that if the power of the laity increases, their own power will decrease. They wish to control and direct the extent of lay involvement by giving assignments to the laity rather than fully involving them in all phases of planning and decision-making about the church's ministry, what should be done, and who should do it.

Pastors who fail to train and equip the laity and then turn them loose to plan and carry out the church's ministry need never expect to build their congregations into truly vital forces for God. They will instead be "people shrinkers," reducing the laity to a point of passive dependence upon them to identify and plan the church's ministry and to assign each lay person a role in it.

Pastors who lead in this way may have a full house every Sunday morning, may raise thousands of dollars for missions and may even have church halls dedicated in their names. The fact remains, however, that if the laity are not actively involved in identifying, planning, and carrying out the ministries of the church they are in some form of slavery to the pastor's leadership, and God will someday have a talk with the pastor about that. God stands absolutely opposed to any type of slavery of His people, whether to Pharaoh or the pastor, even if the people are willing slaves, content with things as they are because they have never had a glimpse of their own potential for ministry and service.

God spoke to Pharoah and said, "Let My people go, that they may serve Me" (Exod. 8:1). Many a sermon has been preached on this text to the effect that Pharaoh and Egypt typify sin, Satan, and all his powers to enslave. The day came when God would tolerate such slavery no longer, and He brought great judgment upon the slave masters.

This text lends itself to another sermon, however. Note that God did not say, "Let My people go that they might serve Moses, whom I have appointed as their new leader and pastor." God wanted the people free to serve Him and Him alone. He stands today equally opposed to all slave-makers whether they are of Satan's league or pastors and leaders in the church. To all alike God says, "Let My people go that they might serve Me. These are My people, not yours." In fact, the entire Bible records God's continuing struggle to free His people from bondage, whether it is to sin, idols, governments, or priests.

THE "LONE RANGER" PASTOR

The type of pastoral leadership we have been describing tends to make the laity into "little tin soldiers" who are all expected to march to the beat of the pastor's drum. There is another type of pastoral leadership that, although it does not so obviously enslave the people, also fails to develop the laity in effective ministries. Those are "Lone Ranger" pastors. The "Pharaoh-type" pastors tend to fashion lay people into robot-like followers who faithfully carry out the pastor's instructions. The Lone Ranger pastor is not interested in getting the people to do anything at all except attend church and contribute largely. He wants to ride off alone to do all the work and, of course, to receive all the attention. The Lone Ranger tends to develop a church program that allows the congregation to sit quietly and watch him as he goes charging by on his way to single-handedly accomplish another great exploit. There will, however, be periodic intermissions designed to allow the otherwise passive congregation ample opportunity to provide the necessary finances for the Lone Ranger's next great exploit.

The Lone Ranger style of pastoral leadership may have been appropriate in former generations, when the pastor was often the only educated person in the community and therefore the only one capable of performing many of the ministries of the church. In such settings the pastor became "Herr pastor," the star performer. Today that is no longer a valid model for pastoral leadership.[1]

An ancient Asian teacher, Lao-Tse (604?-531 B.C.) once described an effective leader:

> A Leader is best when people barely know he exists. Not so good when people obey and acclaim him. Worse when they despise him. But of a good leader who talks little, when his work is done, his aim fulfilled, they will say, "We did it ourselves."

That is the type of leadership needed in the church today. That is the leader God wants you to be. A pastor-leader of this type is most certainly active in the entire affairs of the church, though not as a Pharaoh or a Lone Ranger. This pastor leads much more like a stage manager than a star performer. This pastor steps aside to allow Christ to occupy center stage as the star performer and allows every lay person to fill an important role in the exciting drama of ministry.

That is what true revitalization is all about; Christ, pastor, and people working together, each filling his proper role in planning and carrying out the ministry of the church.[2]

The pastor's role in all of this is absolutely vital and foundational. That role is to identify, recruit, train, and equip the laity to do the work God is calling them to do. That is precisely what Paul was referring to when he said God had called some "as pastors and teachers, for the equipping of the saints for the work of service" (Eph. 4:12). It is not for the pastor to make all the decisions and to do all the work, but to equip the saints. It is by equipping alone that the pastor will ever succeed in the "building up of the body of Christ . . . according to the proper working of each individual part" (Eph. 4:12-16).

As every pastor knows, that is no easy task. It is, however, one of his most important responsibilities. If the pastor fails to equip the saints, they will never be equipped. They will remain slaves to their own limitations and inabilities, the church will not be revitalized, and the work of God will suffer.

In order to equip the people, the pastor and church need an ongoing, long-range program for identifying, recruiting, training, and assigning lay leaders and workers to their respective places of service in the church's ministries. Following is a plan that may help you to do this.

A PROCEDURE FOR DEVELOPING LAY LEADERS

I. Establish a clear and unique purpose for each program in the church.
II. Identify and recruit lay persons who have the abilities to fulfill the purposes.
III. Develop a ministry covenant that spells out the expectations of the task of each lay worker.
IV. Train and equip the workers to do the task in a satisfactory manner.
V. Provide necessary support and supervision.

We will now discuss each of those steps in more detail, attempting to give you some ideas about how you may begin identifying and developing lay leaders in your church.

I. *Establish a clear and unique purpose for each program in the church.*

We discussed earlier the need for a church to be clear about its own mission, that which God is calling it to be and do. Just so must each program or ministry in the church also have a clear sense of its own purpose; that is, how it by doing its task enables the church to fulfill its larger mission.

We suggest you give the church's mission statement to each program committee in the church, asking them to consider what part their particular program plays in fulfilling that mission. To help the committees get at this, ask each of them to respond to the following questions:

1. What is the unique purpose of the program for which we are specifically responsible? What specific ministry do we carry out that no other group in the church is intended to do?
2. What important aspects of our church's ministry will be left undone if we do not do them?
3. How do our specific program responsibilities support the church's mission statement?
4. Specifically, what skills, knowledge, and resources do we need in order to fulfill our purpose as we have described it? Which of those do we now have? Which do we not now have?

After the existing program committees have prepared their responses to the above questions, have representatives from each committee meet with the administrative board to answer the following questions:

1. Are there gaps in our total ministry? Are important areas or activities not being done by any program or committee?
2. Are there overlaps? Is there any ministry area or activity that is being covered by more than one program or committee?
3. What adjustments are necessary in any of these purpose statements to close a gap, reduce an overlap, and assure that if every committee accomplishes its purpose, the congregation's mission will be fulfilled?
4. What additional program ministries do we suggest for our church? What skills, knowledge and resources will each of those new ministries require?

After the above work is completed you are ready to:

II. *Identify and recruit lay persons who have the abilities to fulfill the purposes of each program ministry in your church.*

This is a crucial step in the life and ministry of any church, and most churches do it poorly by having a group or the pastor alone hurriedly put together a list of nominees a few days before the annual business meeting. Often the questions dealt with by that group do not deal with purposes, skills, or resources at all. About the most significant questions asked are, "Who did this job last year?" and "Do you think we can talk him into it for another year?" Even worse, those committees often give important jobs to people who have not been attending church at all; "If we give him this job, he'll have to start coming." They reward a person for his lack of interest in the church, and almost certainly doom a program to failure. There is a better way for your church to go about identifying and recruiting leaders!

We suggest that your church carefully appoint a nominating-personnel committee that works on a regular basis, year around, to identify areas in which workers are needed, recruit persons to fill those needs, provide for all necessary training and resourcing of the workers, and conduct evaluation and feedback sessions to workers on the effectiveness of their programs.[3]

We suggest the nominating-personnel committee go about its important task of recruiting lay workers in the following manner:

A. Prepare a description of each leadership position in the church.
   1. Define the purpose of the program for which leadership will be offered. (Most of this will have been done in the earlier work of the program committees and the board.)
   2. List the responsibilities and tasks the person is to fulfill. Be as specific as possible.
   3. List the necessary skills, knowledge, and resources the persons will need to do the job well.
   4. Estimate realistically the time that will need be given to the task, including preparation and study.
   5. Suggest ways that training could be provided if the person being recruited does not possess the necessary skills and knowledge.

   The information describing each job is prepared as a "Ministry Covenant," which includes a place for the signature of the person who will finally accept the task and for the signatures of the board's chairperson and the pastor.

B. Conduct a leadership study of the congregation to determine the previous experience, skills, and knowledge of each member. Also list the programs and ministries each member has interest in as possible areas of service.

C. Recruit the persons most qualified to fill each position.

Questions to be considered are:
1. Does this person have the ability to do the job well? If not how will we provide the necessary training and support to ensure their success?
2. Does this person have sufficient time to give to the job?
3. Does this person have sufficient interest in the job?

Some important principles to be followed in recruiting workers are:
1. Personally visit, perhaps at least twice, each person to be recruited. The first visit is to review the job description and ascertain a possible interest. The second is to obtain a response for filling the position. Training should be discussed during both visits.
2. Present to the annual meeting for election only the names of those persons who have indicated a willingness to serve, to receive any necessary training, and who have signed a "Ministry Covenant." The covenant is described below.

III. *Develop a ministry covenant that spells out the expectations of the task of each lay worker.*

The ministry covenant contains the description of the position and the responsibilities that go with it plus any other specific agreements the individual and the nominating-personnel may have reached during the recruiting visits. In addition there is a place for the signatures of the worker, administrative board chairperson, (or other appropriate lay officer), and the pastor.

By signing the ministry covenant the worker agrees to fulfill the expectations of the task. The signature of the board's chairperson pledges the church to provide the necessary resources and training to do the job. The pastor's signature signals his commitment to provide moral support, supervision, and spiritual counsel to the worker and the congregation as they join together in ministry.

IV. *Train and equip the workers to do the task in a satisfactory manner.*

Often recruiting a willing lay worker is only half the job. Unless the person possesses the necessary skills to do the job, willingness is not enough. A willing but unskilled worker will soon become discouraged. Training is therefore the key to releasing the potential for ministry that each worker has.

If any person recruited to a task in the church does not already have the necessary skills to be a success, due to previous training or experience, the pastor and church are morally responsible to provide that person with such training.

Evangelical churches discovered the secret of training Sunday school workers several decades ago. As a result evangelical denominations have developed supurb training materials for Sunday school officers and teachers. Those materials have been used in the local churches to train and equip the finest cadre of Sunday school workers the Christian church has ever seen. Has all of this effort to train the workers paid off? Absolutely! Today, and for the past several years, evangelical Sunday schools are growing at an unprecedented rate, while at the same time the Sunday schools of nonevangelical churches have been shrinking at an unprecedented rate. The nonevangelical denominations have put as much money and effort into providing Sunday school literature and classrooms, but that was not enough. The one thing they have generally failed to do is provide consistent, effective training for their workers.

Training made the difference for evangelical Sunday schools. But a great many evangelical pastors and leaders have not learned that lesson when it comes to other church programs and they are paying a price for their non-learning. Again and again pastors complain to us about ineffective youth programs, unsupportive board members, disagreeable committee chairpersons, choir directors. Yet when we ask them regarding the type and quality of training they have provided for those workers their response generally is, "I have never even thought about the need to train them."

Because such material is already in print we will not write more about training here, but urge you to study the following books: *Let My People Go: Empowering Laity for Minstry* by Lindgren and Shawchuck and *Dry Bones Breathe* by Worley.[4]

V. *Provide necessary support and supervision.*

The most important support the congregation can possibly give is to consistently pray for the lay ministers in public and in private. Any caring pastor and congregation will develop a prayer program in which every worker is prayed for every day.

In addition, the lay workers need continuous supervisory

support as they carry out their ministries. The pastor must remain in touch with them, offering encouragement and counsel and seeing to it that each one has the necessary resources for his job. In addition there are several specific ways in which the pastor and congregation can express support for the workers.

A. A Commissioning Ceremony

Remember the ministry covenant that each worker signed? Each of those covenants can be put into an attractive, inexpensive frame to be presented to the workers in a public service in which the congregation gathers to recognize, pray for, and commission the workers to carry out their ministries in the name of Christ and on behalf of the congregation.

It is well for the pastor to build the entire service around the theme "the priesthood of all believers" and to preach about the call of God to lay persons, which makes them "priests and workers for Christ Jesus."

It might be well to have two or three of the workers speak about their own hopes in the job they have accepted and of their excitement to be able to serve God and the church in this way. Then, with all of the workers at the altar, and the congregation in the pews, the Lord's supper may be served. Finally, the church board may join the pastor in laying hands on the workers and commissioning them to their tasks.

You may wish to invite the religious editor of your local newspaper, or someone from the local television news staff to attend the commissioning service and report on it through their new medium.

B. Meaningful Rewards

Generally the church is woefully lax and its leaders are grossly uncreative when it comes to providing lay workers with appropriate and meaningful rewards for their work. Of course, the workers do not expect to be paid for their work and they know that by their faithful service they are "laying up treasures for themselves in heaven." Nonetheless, we have never yet found a worker who did not deeply appreciate and who was not motivated by appropriate and meaningful rewards for his faithfulness. Again, the Sunday schools know something about this.

For many years, hundreds of our Sunday schools presented a "Sunday school pin" for each year of faithful attendance. Thousands of students collected and proudly displayed their pins; for five, ten, twenty years and more. Times changed and there came a day when many Sunday schools, and many students, began to feel the meager little pins were no longer as appropriate or meaningful. Hundreds of schools discontinued their use, and thousands of students were found to be no longer as faithful. Was that simply because the schools stopped giving the pins? No, it was because the schools never replaced them with another reward system that would be appropriate for our modern, more affluent Sunday school students.

A wise pastor and church will search constantly to provide each worker with rewards that are:

1. Appropriate for the specific ministry the worker is doing.
2. Personally meaningful to the individual. This may often require effort and mind stretching! A certain reward may be appropriate but not meaningful to the individual, and vice versa. This being the case, it may be that the church will not be able to find one type of reward that will be satisfactory for all the workers. This is exactly what happened in the case of the Sunday school attendance pins. They remained an appropriate reward for faithful attendance, and they were still meaningful to many students, as evidenced by their no longer being quite so faithful when they no longer received them. For many other students, however, they had become unmeaningful (after all, what is a cheap little pin in a day of motor-bikes, color televisions, and Hawaii vacations?) and therefore unappreciated.

   Should the schools have kept using them because of the few who still found them meaningful, or were they right in discontinuing them because of the many who no longer found meaning in them? Neither answer is fully satisfactory.

Perhaps the answer is that the schools should have kept

using them with students who yet found them meaningful and should have found other appropriate rewards for the students for whom the pins had lost meaning. If the schools made any error it was, and is, in assuming it should give only one type of reward for faithful attendance.

This concept holds fully true when it comes to rewarding workers for their service. What one Sunday school may find to be a meaningful reward may be empty of meaning for another, and what may prove to be appropriate for a Sunday school teacher may be an inappropriate reward for the organist.

Many pastors know this whole business of rewarding volunteer workers is complex and time consuming, and for that reason many churches choose to ignore the issue altogether. But providing appropriate and meaningful rewards can play a major role in sustaining the enthusiasm and dedication of your workers. Whatever effort and cost you put into providing appropriate and meaningful rewards will pay big dividends in terms of motivation, faithfulness, and gratitude on the part of your workers.

Because the rewards you give must be selected in the light of the ministry and the workers, we cannot give you a complete reward system. We can, however, suggest a few to stimulate your own thinking.

How about providing organ lessons for the organist, or buying a ticket to an organ recital, which you present to him or her with a hearty thanks in a public worship service?

How about rewarding each Sunday school teacher with a Ryrie Study Bible? This might be done in the middle of the church school year, and, of course, in a public service. Some teachers might be asked to share exciting highlights of their teaching experience.

How about rewarding the church board members with a weekend spiritual life retreat? It might be held in the fall of the year, at a beautiful, comfortable lodge where the people can enjoy a weekend of nature's beauty and spiritual growth. You might also ask them to bring their spouses or a special friend as a double reward. For a retreat leader you might invite a denominational representative, a retired pastor, or a seminary professor.

How about rewarding the church janitor with a special recognition service in which you present him with a dustpan on which is painted, "Cleanliness is next to godliness, and your work makes it easier for all people to find Him here." Chances are he'll proudly hang the dustpan in his house for all to see!

C. Provide feedback on how well the workers are doing.

Leaders need and want feedback on how well they are doing. Most pastors shy away from giving any feedback, especially if the worker is doing poorly. Many of those same pastors, however, will not hestitate to complain about those workers to other pastors or to other church members and sometimes even to God. Such complaining is damaging and sinful.[5] Instead, the pastor and nominating-personnel committee should set up a structure to examine how workers and programs are doing. This information should be given to the workers so they might rejoice in their areas of strength and improve in their areas of weakness.

Many pastors are fearful such assessment will threaten the workers, but the fact is that many will feel supported by it and will rejoice that their job merits the church's notice.

D. A Recognition Celebration

All lay people appreciate a public recognition for a job well done. Just as we urge a ceremony to commission a worker to a new ministry, so we urge a service to recognize and celebrate the completion of the assignment.

The pastor and congregation should never miss an opportunity to celebrate. Celebration is a vital key to a revitalized church. Sadly, few pastors recognize this. Some even feel that to praise lay people for their faithful service and to celebrate it in public service is somehow sinful. Pastors who avoid festive, appropriate celebration in the services must somehow read the psalms with a special set of filters. How else could they fail to see the often-repeated admonitions to make worship a joyful, festive, happy celebration? Consider the words of David (Psalm 150):

> Praise the Lord!
> Praise God in His sanctuary;
> Praise Him in His mighty
>   expanse.
>
> Praise Him for His mighty deeds;
> Praise Him according to His
>   excellent greatness.
>
> Praise Him with trumpet sound;
> Praise Him with harp and lyre.
>
> Praise Him with timbrel and
>   dancing;
> Praise Him with stringed instruments
>   and pipe.
>
> Praise Him with loud cymbals;
> Praise Him with resounding cymbals.
>
> Let everything that has breath praise
>   the Lord.
>
> Praise the Lord!

About what should the congregation become so excited that the people simply cannot help but clap, dance for joy, and "beat the drums?" For all the great work God is doing, certainly! But should the congregation be not equally excited about all the great work the lay workers are doing? Certainly! For God has now chosen to do much of His great work through them. When we celebrate their work we celebrate His work. When we ignore their work we ignore His work. When we praise them for ministry offered to others, we praise God for His ministry offered to us.

Conclusion

Here, then, are seven keys to developing a corps of vital, committed lay ministers in your church:
1. Recruit willing workers who will covenant to faithfully do their ministry as "unto the Lord."

2. Train them and provide all the necessary resources to do their job well.
3. Commission them to minister on behalf of the entire congregation.
4. Provide them with constant prayer support and supervision.
5. Reward each worker with appropriate and meaningful rewards.
6. Provide helpful feedback on how well the workers and programs are doing.
7. Seize every opportunity to celebrate the work and accomplishments of each and every lay worker.

A church is made up of its people and their ministry. Therefore, if a church is ever to be revitalized it must experience that revitalization in the lives and ministries of its members. The steps for developing lay leaders and workers we have outlined in this chapter require hard work and creativity on the part of the pastor, we know. For that reason, and because they are threatened by a powerful laity, many pastors are very reluctant to do what we suggest in this chapter and throughout this book.

But until you begin to *work* in this manner you will never have a revitalized church. You may plead, beg, and even threaten the congregation, and one or two persons may wake up and get busy. You may have a group or two in your church that is vibrant and alive; you may even have a revival meeting once a year to try to awaken the sleeping (dying?) members. The fact remains, however, that the only road to a truly vital, active, powerful congregation is one by which you enable the members, all of them, to assess their interests and opportunities for ministry, develop a clear sense of mission for their church, and plan the strategies and programs by which they (not the pastor alone) will achieve their mission and ministry. That will be a start, but not enough. You will need to go on to recruit, prepare, and commission faithful and effective lay ministers into every area of the church's ministry. You will need to consistently involve the entire congregation in all of this in every possible way. For the only way to revitalize a church is to work with the entire congregation, to bring them all along at the same time. Any lesser effort will produce lesser results. It may revitalize a group or one department of the church. It may even bring a spark of new life to the entire congregation, but only for a short while.

There are no shortcuts to revitalizing your church.

In chapters 1-4 we have presented a comprehensive plan for engaging the entire congregation in planning and carrying out the church's ministry. Revitalizing a twentieth century church requires that the entire congregation and all of its committees be involved in the process all at once. Fads and themes will not do. Only sustained, comprehensive efforts that seek to bring new direction and vitality to all groups simultaneously has much hope of working in today's congregations of better educated, more active and autonomous laity.

It is not too difficult to plot the attempts of the American church to renew itself, almost decade by decade. The themes may vary somewhat from denomination to denomination, but the general trends can probably be plotted as follows:

1920s	Revivalism
1930s	Social Gospel
1940s	Sunday School
1950s	Church Buildings
1960s	Social Action
1970s	Church Growth/Body Life

Each emphasis is picked up and becomes the dominant theme of the church's efforts to revitalize itself. Then, after about ten years, people realize that the theme, like all others before it, is no panacea for the problems confronting the church. The church then casts the theme aside in search for another.

In the preceding chapters we have advocated no single theme. Rather, we have advocated a comprehensive approach to planning and organizing that allows the entire congregation, and all of its committees, to combine all of its resources in the pursuit of goals and programs that will move the entire church (not merely a part of it) toward renewed vitality.

The preceding chapters constitute a discrete, complete section of this book. Read by themselves they present a complete planning cycle and the necessary organizational structures and volunteer resources to carry out the plans. There are, however, a number of aspects within the life of the congregation that have vital influence upon the subjects discussed in the first section of this book:

> Financial Aspects of Revitalization
> Relational Aspects of Revitalization
> Missional Aspects of Revitalization
> Proclamational Aspects of Revitalization

After discussing those aspects of congregation revitalization, we will reflect theologically on the various processes for revitalizing a congregation that are discussed throughout this book.

NOTES

1. For an in-depth discussion of the effects of your leadership upon the church and its ministry read Alvin J. Lindgrin and Norman Shawchuck, *Let My People Go: Empowering Laity for Ministry* (Nashville: Abingdon, 1980). See also Norman Shawchuck, *Taking A Look at Your Leadership Styles* (Organization Resources Press, 1977).
2. For an exciting account of how one pastor is succeeding in enabling the laity to fill their roles in ministry, read Jerry Cook, *Love, Acceptance and Forgiveness* (Glendale, Calif.: Gospel Light, Regal, 1979).
3. For a helpful discussion on the functioning of a nominating-personnel committee see Lindgren and Shawchuck, *Let My People Go*, and Norman Shawchuck, "The Local Church: Who Works for Whom?" *Leadership*, Winter 1980.
4. Robert Worley, *Dry Bones Breathe* (Center for the Study of Church Organizational Behavior, 1978).
5. Dietrich Bonhoeffer says God never called the pastor to complain about the congregation, and it is a sin to do so, even if the pastor cloaks the complaining in prayer. See Dietrich Bonhoeffer, *Life Together*, trans. John W. Doberstein (New York: Harper & Row, 1954), pp. 29-30, 92.

5

Financial Aspects of Revitalization

The way the church gathers and spends its money and all other resources will most certainly work for or against revitalization. Disagreement over money and its use is a primary cause of many church fights. It is imperative therefore that any effort to revitalize the church include a good hard look at the financial procedures of the church.

When we talk about money and budgets, we are talking about the same subjects discussed in the planning chapter. This chapter does not deal with a totally new subject; it deals with the same material from a different perspective. Goal-setting results in a *qualitative* statement of the church program. The budget of the church is a *quantitative* statement of that same program. Both statements should say the same basic thing about the mission of the church and the direction in which the church wants to go.

The budget-building process itself should be a revitalizing process. It should reflect the mind of God for the program of the church, not merely the conglomerate opinion of the people regarding how cheaply they can operate the church for another year. How different this is from the usual budgeting procedure in which the budget is hurriedly and begrudgingly built by a few people who ask:

1. What did it cost to keep the door open last year?
2. How little can we increase the pastor's salary and still keep him happy?
3. How much must we add for inflation?

This chapter deals with the church program from the point of view of church budgeting, accounting, and reporting procedures that breathe life into financial procedures of the church and further the vision of the people to support the program of the church.

BUILDING THE BUDGET

There is a correlation between the faithful use of money and the quality of the congregation's spiritual life. Martin Luther said, "There are three conversions: the conversion of the heart, the mind and the purse." Money talks. What is it saying about your church and its program?

David McConaughty authored a book, *Money, the Acid Test*, around the turn of the century in which he said that money, the most common of temporal things, involves uncommon and eternal consequences.[1] In the process of getting, saving, using, giving, and accounting for it money molds churches and people. Money can prove to be a blessing or a curse. A person can become master of money or money can be the master of the person. It also can master the congregation. Money will buy a building but not a church.

The problems, patterns, and potential of individual financial conditions have an effect upon the church. The point of view the pastor and his people have toward raising and spending money in connection with the church will have much to do with the effectiveness of the entire church ministry. Budgets and how they are built can be a very real and vital part of the revitalization of a church.

The public has a right to expect churches to not only live within their financial means but also to set an example of good financial management as well. Spiritually sound money-raising, careful budgeting, accurate record-keeping, and reporting that accounts not only for dollars but for ministries should characterize our church financial programs.

All of the business functions of a congregation have something to say to the community. The silent message that comes from those activities should be bold and clear. It should convey the truth that here is an important organization. It is an organization that knows what it is trying to do and knows how to do it. It is an organization that goes about its business in a serious manner. If fully recognizes its goals and is concerned about the welfare of its neighbors. It is evident through the budget that the church is in full support of the goals and programs established by the people for the church.

In the earlier chapters of this book we stressed the necessity of involving the entire congregation in establishing the mission, goals, and programs of the church. Once that is done, the congregation should be given an opportunity to underwrite its goals and programs with its time and money. Good church planning, therefore, will naturally include a budgeting process that clearly shows the connection between the congregation's goals and the budget and demonstrates how support of the budget will bring the congregation's hopes and dreams into reality.

PROGRAM BUDGET

The church budget, if it is to assist in revitalizing the congregation, must clearly talk about the very same goals and programs the congregation set for itself in the planning process. Unless the people can see the connection between their goals and the budget they can hardly be expected to support the budget.

The budget, then, should be stated in terms of goals and programs—a *program budget*. The program budget is a forecast of anticipated income and expenses for a defined future period that shows how specific programs will be supported by the money contributed to the church.

To serve effectively as a plan for spending, the budget should, first, reflect the congregation's goals and programs. Every department, large or small, should have an opportunity to have its needs considered and included. It lists estimated costs, for example, for the activities of the minister, the educational program, the church office, and building and grounds maintenance. It is the function of a budget to attach a dollar-and-cents value to each of the programs of the church.

Second, the budget should be equitable. Funds should be allocated in such a way that each department can accomplish the purposes the congregation wants it to accomplish. Third, it should be capable of change. When emergencies arise, departments should cooperate to bring about a revision of the budget. That may mean curtailing or postponing expenditures or activities so that funds originally allocated for one department can be made available to another department. Fourth, it should be attainable. A church council reviews a proposed budget and refers requests back to the department if the total budget becomes unattainable. Fifth, the budget should be challenging. The need of the church's programs should determine the amount of money requested.

Financial budgets serve two purposes. They can serve as a guide for spending or as an instrument for the control of spending. A budget can be developed and used autocratically or democratically. It can be a rigid, unbending master or a helpful servant.

The basic plan for formulating a budget can be divided into five distinct steps: planning, programming, education, response, and evaluation. Planning, which has been set forth in chapters 1 and 2, includes the gathering of facts, trends, and statistical data that will be useful in developing the program of the church. It is information that will tell the story of what has gone on before, where the congregation has been, and how it has responded in the past. Although such statistics will note trends, they are not intended to forecast future performance. The details are laid out, the facts are gathered, leaders are chosen as indicated in chapter 3, and the plan begins to unfold. The process is under way.

As the process continues, the plans are formulated into programs and the cost of each program is determined. The costs of the various programs are collected to make up the church budget.

The fund-raising program then procedes to the education step. All of the statistical information on the congregation's past performance, the potential giving determined by a representative group of members, and the proposed program to fit those resources and extend the mission of the church must be communicated. Somebody has to tell the people all about it. It is the education committee whose job it now is to tell the story.

A plan is developed and implemented to teach mission and Christian giving, to tell the people how it is now and how it can be in the future. That is accomplished through a variety of ways and means with the use of every available media—letters, visual aids, posters, broadsides, bulletins, speeches, one-to-one conversation—to bring understanding and involvement in the life of the church.

Perhaps small group discussions using the same group who gathered for the assessment (see chapter 1) can be invited to a second home meeting in which the entire program of the church is explained: the statistics, the giving potential, and the proposed program. Discussion flows freely. Questions are answered. Confidence is improved, fellowship is enhanced, inspiration abounds. Dedicated members go home to discuss their own plans for giving.

Instead of group discussions in the home, one big happy joyous congregational dinner, perhaps catered, could bring as many or more people together for an even more elaborate presentation: big charts, movies, multi-media visual projections, recorded sound programs, skits and speeches.

When you have gathered the facts, developed a program proposal, and told the members all about it, you are ready for the crucial moment: the all-important response. This fourth step is accomplished through visits to every member and the final tally of pledges so received. More people will respond this way than in any other way.

Throughout the year monthly reports are given showing ministries and goals accomplished and budgets expended, with much celebration for the accomplishments.

Step 5 puts the final wrap-up on the program. This is an evaluation of what has been done, what could have been done better, and what should be done next time around. The evaluation process is discussed in chapter 2 as the fifth step in the planning cycle.

A budget is more than just dollar signs and columns of numbers on a sheet of paper. It reflects the life of the congregation. It is the financial expression of its programs, priorities, and dreams stated in down-to-earth terms of dollars and cents. The congregation wants to see the connection between its goals and the budget. People tend to support what they have helped to create.[2]

A *program budget* is the approach we recommend for budgeting and reporting. It offers a significant opportunity for creative planning and spending. Such budgets are organized to reflect the costs of programs rather than items of expense. All costs required for a particular program are identified with that program. A conventional church budget can be transformed into a program or planning budget. We put rather realistic price tags on each goal and program the congregation has set for itself.

When using such a budget, the cost of a specific program can be measured to determine its effectiveness by asking what has been accomplished. The pastor's salary, for example, is divided proportionately among those programs in which pastoral leadership is involved. The cost of office supplies is allocated to those programs requiring such supplies.

Program budgets begin by establishing a need and by setting goals as demonstrated in chapters 1 and 2. Then programs are described which will fulfill those needs and achieve those goals. The form of the budget becomes important as a tool for planning and decision-making, for evaluation and for communication. Although costs are still clearly shown and detailed for all expenditures, they focus in on fulfilling the life and mission of the congregation in programs.

LINE ITEM BUDGET

The budget probably most frequently used in congregations is the *line item budget*. That is a budget that lists, line by line, the dollars to be spent on expense items; salaries, utilities, benevolences, evangelism, Sunday school, church, time, insurance, mortgage payments, nursery care, repairs, and so on. Each line item is carefully defined, costs estimated and amount budgeted.

Unfortunately the line item budget makes no attempt to show how the budget supports the church's program, such things as education, spiritual formation, worship. The line item budget talks about such things as insurance, salaries, lawnmowers. For this reason we suggest you make every effort to learn the basic principles of program budgeting, and that you apply those principles to the budgeting process of your church.

However, even though you use program budgeting, the line item budget will remain an essential tool for your treasurer and the finance committee as they monitor the actual expenditures of your church's money. The program budget does not replace the line item budget; it is used along with the line item budget.

SUPPORTING THE BUDGET

There are dangers connected with designated giving. Popular items in the budget will be over-pledged, and items that are necessary but not as popular will go wanting. It is more

Financial Aspects of Revitalization • 81

glamorous to designate money for the support of the missionary on the field than it is to provide transportation for him to reach the field. Administrative expenses are necessary but are not glamour items in the budget and therefore do not attract designations. People will gladly support administration when they see its connection with the programs and vision. It is preferable to have a budget formulated that all can support and then contribute to that budget without designations. It is encouraging to note that there is a comparatively low administrative cost in the church. The average is about 9 percent, compared to 67 percent in the federal government, 51 percent in the state government, and 27 percent in city and county governments.

It is wise to print on the budget the principles of finance that have been adopted by the church. When they are so noted, they can be carried from year to year and will not get lost in the books of the minutes.

Lyle Schaller has an interesting list of financial principles that he discusses in connection with his work in a Lutheran parish.[7] The first is that the budget should be presented to people in terms of needs the members will understand. The one presenting the budget should avoid abstractions. A second principle is to listen to people rather than to merely exhort them to give. The next principle says that the local church tends to reflect each member's perception of need, the quality of internal communication, and the degree of the member's involvement in the life, program, and ministry of that congregation. It does that far more than it reflects the financial capability of the commitment or the loyalty of each member.

The fourth principle states that people respond to real needs when they become aware of them. The next reminds us that a few years ago people would contribute to the church simply out of loyalty, whereas today they want to know how the money is going to be used. We are reminded that two-way communication is superior to one-way communication, which means that feedback is beneficial. The seventh principle states that we must increase the volume and quality of our communication with the people on financial matters to match the progress that has been developed in communication in other areas. When talking to people about church finances, we should begin with their needs, not with trying to encourage them to feel an interest in solving our financial problems. The longer a local church delays beginning to plan for its finances, the fewer the open options and the lower the chances of a satisfactory outcome from the planning efforts. Financial programs are limited by the traditions, values, attitudes, and practices of each local church.

Some additional principles might include the encouragement to reduce financial machinery to a minimum while still keeping accurate records. The needs and opportunities for ministry of the church should be presented directly to the church. People enjoy giving to what they can see. The money raised should only be expended when the bills have been checked by authorized personnel in the church. The financial records should be audited on a regular basis.

To be most effective every church communication system should include a monthly mailing report of both giving and non-giving to every member of the parish. Experience in a wide variety of parishes across the nation has indicated that the monthly reporting system increases recorded giving by at least 12 percent.

Five items should be included in every monthly mailing:
1. A report of the progress made on the goals of the church and how finances have helped make that possible.
2. A copy of the monthly giving form.
3. A stewardship education leaflet selected to emphasize one aspect of the church's program.
4. A report from the treasurer showing the income and expenditures for the month just past.
5. A personally signed mimeographed letter concerning the major program emphasis for the coming month and accomplishments of the month just past.

Sending only a financial statement often results in negative comments and phone calls to the church office. The importance of reporting to both givers and non-givers alike cannot be stressed too strongly.

This reporting system will result in a better informed parish, a higher degree of stewardship motivation among the members, more involvement of members in the work of the church, and ultimately greater income for God's work.

All churches, regardless of their denominational affiliations, should end their fiscal years with the calendar year. Experience has shown that the income for the months of June, July, and August will, because of members' vacations, be below the average monthly sums needed as income for the year. If the fiscal year of a church begins in June, the church is unable at the beginning of the year to pay all bills in full. That tends to limit the program and creates a negative outlook on the part of the boards and congregation. When a church begins its fiscal year January 1, it will receive more than half of its yearly income during the first six months of the year.

Financial aspects are important to the process of revitalization. That importance can be emphasized by having the church celebrate each major financial step taken and each financial victory gained. The people waited upon God for His direction. He provided the means for achieving the goals and carrying out the planning process. A spiritual celebration should mark each financial victory.

Further Thoughts Regarding the Budget

Since a budget is a plan for carrying out the wish of the people, the contents of the plan must come from the people. After the budget has been adopted, it becomes the official plan for spending the money of a congregation, the tool that guides a budget-control officer in his spending.

When the need for major budget changes arises during the year (e.g. more than $100 within a single department), those should be considered and approved by the same people who worked out the budget. That way a budget expresses the will of the people of a congregation. The people can therefore be expected to support it and exert every possible effort to meet it.

It may seem that a budget controls only money, but in reality it controls the decisions and actions of the people who spend the money. A budget should not only express the composite plan of the people of a congregation, but it should also control those people when it comes to spending the money of the church. A system of reports to people who spend church funds helps them keep their expenditures within the limits of a budget. Such reports are given in detail to the chairman of each department. When a budget does not provide for a given expenditure, the congregation must give its permission in some other way to spend its money outside budget provisions.

By the time a congregation reaches the second or third quarter of a fiscal year, it can usually tell whether it will be able to stay within its budget. If it is doubtful that it can, it should make budget adjustments by adjusting programs. There are only two possible ways to take care of expenditures beyond a budget allocation: obtain more money to make spending beyond original plans possible, or reduce the budget of one department to enable another department to get more money. Although the need for adjusting a budget is to be expected and is not necessarily an admission of error or inefficiency, such adjustments should be held to a minimum.

The budgeting procedure we are suggesting here will help you avoid the many dangers inherent in the "dream budget" that many congregations use to their own harm year after year. The "dream budget" is the one formulated the last minute before the annual meeting by one individual to whom the task was assigned to bring in a budget. With no careful planning and input by the program agencies of the church, the best the person can do is put together a "dream sheet." This is a far cry from presenting the congregation with an actual workable budget. Presenting your congregation with a budget is not a game, and it should reflect something more than a dream. Be serious about planning, presenting, and following the budget—or don't do it at all.

CONCLUSION

A budget is a statement of purpose and a diagram of expectations. It is a plan that specifies goals, puts price tags on the goals and shows how to reach them. It is a precedent for future decisions and a basis for evaluation. The members have a right to know what is included in the budget and the progress being made toward meeting it. This type of budgeting is almost certain to revitalize the giving, indeed all of the stewardship practices, of your church. (See Appendix C for a brief manual of church accounting principles.)

NOTES

1. Howard L. Dayton, Jr., *Your Money: Frustration or Freedom?* (Wheaton, Ill.: Tyndale, 1971), pp. 13-15.
2. For an in-depth discussion of the budgeting process described here, see Alvin J. Lindgrin and Norman Shawchuck, *Management for Your Church: How to Realize Your Church Potential Through Systems Approach* (Nashville: Abingdon, 1977), especially chapter 6, "The Program Planning and Budgeting Systems," pp. 79-100.

6

Relational Aspects of Revitalization

Depersonalization is one of the characteristic processes of our day. Social security numbers have taken the place of names of people. Schools design educational programs for the masses and have a tendency to overlook individual differences of the students. The church must not adopt this common philosophical approach. Programs must never be considered apart from people. When God revitalizes His church, He will do it through people, not buildings.

The Bible does not emphasize processes apart from people. There are 2,930 different people specifically named within the sixty-six books of Scripture. A constructive approach to church revitalization must also emphasize people as well as processes. In the introduction and throughout the chapters of the book, we have been referring to church leaders, parishioners, pastors, small groups, and maturing believers. Church leadership is not born, it is developed. Small groups cannot carry out constructive work in the process of revitalization unless there is some cohesiveness in the group and an ability evidenced among its members of being able to get along together. In developing the process of revitalization within a church the individuals must not only be concerned with maintaining a good vertical relationship with God but also with maintaining good horizontal relationships with those with whom they are working. This is a fact often overlooked by pastors and people alike.

Someone has written, "To dwell above with saints we love, O that will be glory; to dwell below, with saints we know, O that's another story!" The story goes that there were two porcupines living in northern Canada. They realized that if they were to keep warm, it would be necessary for them to get close together. However, each time they got together they kept needling one another. That may be a modern parable of some of our church situations.

It has been said that 90 percent of all people who fail in their life's vocations fail because they cannot get along with people. Many church executives responsible for the oversight of pastors tell us the number one problem facing pastors today is that they do not know how to get along with people. Some years ago a survey was made in Chicago attempting to discover the interests of adults who wanted to pursue advanced education. It was discovered that their primary interest was in course work related to the maintenance of good health. Their second choice of course work and training was in the area of skills in human relationships.[1] They had lived long enough to realize the necessity of knowing how to get along with people. Any pastor who wants to be fully successful in ministering had better learn that lesson also.

The necessity for developing skills in human relationships is especially noted in the area of church work, including the revitalization process. God did not create people as "tools" for the church. The church exists to serve people and not vice versa. On the other hand, the church cannot do its work without the cooperation and involvement of the people. They possess the resources the church needs to minister both to the congregation itself and to the world beyond. That dependence upon the support and cooperation of people poses some serious challenges to leaders. People come in many shapes and sizes and often do not fit perfectly into the leader's plans. People have ideas of their own and their own goals for the church. They often disagree among themselves and with the leaders. Peter Drucker, in *The Effective Executive,* also reminds us that people do not come in the proper size and shape for tasks that have to be done in organizations. They are almost-fits at best. In spite of that the leaders must learn to get along with people to bring them all along together as the church moves forward in its ministry.

Dr. Samuel Blizzard, in his doctoral dissertation at Pennsylvania State University, stirred up quite a storm in circles when he reminded us that a pastor on the average spends nine hours and fifty-seven minutes on the job seven days a week. Three hours and fifty-seven minutes of that time is spent in administration, which is more time on the average than he spends in carrying out his pastoral duties. He spends one hour and ten minutes on the average as an organizer, which is more time than he spends as a teacher. In surveying such statistics as those we have become aware once again of the importance of developing good interpersonal relationships. It is in the context of dealing with people in organizations that most of our ministry is done.

This chapter is designed to provide some help in understanding people, relating to others, working together, leading people, and maturing as individuals. The church will never be revitalized apart from its constituency. We must provide help for the people if we would improve the process. The relational aspects of revitalization are important.

Understanding People

It is important for those involved in the process of revitalization to be able to understand people. Their idiosyncracies must be recognized and their strengths and weaknesses evaluated with fairness. A pastor must be able to discern the spiritual levels his people have attained and the additional steps they need to take toward maturity. Unfortunately, some in the church who may feel that they are spiritual giants are not always the most cooperative.

The process of revitalization involves the evaluation and allocation of board and committee activities. There are times when one person can obstruct the progress of the entire group. Effective skills in group process and conflict management are especially needed at this point so that the obstruction can be corrected or removed. The removal of an obstructionist can be a cataclysmic experience. Many churches suffer from the effects of obstructionists simply because the pastor does not know how to effectively lead in the context of opposition.

We must recognize and admit that all people are different. Within the realm of management the different person is often referred to as a problem person. If that were actually true, then each person would be a problem. The individual may not conform to all of the standards of the group in behavior, attitude, and dress but that does not necessarily mean that he is a problem person. Such a nonconforming individual does not automatically threaten group unity or effectiveness. We must view people from their position and not from our own. We are all acting and reacting within different environments. We should seek to understand and evaluate people on the basis of truth rather than on the basis of personal preference. That is important if we are aiming to involve as many people as possible in the revitalization process.

It is important not only to understand others but also to understand ourselves in relationship to those with whom we relate. There are basically three reasons why self-awareness is intricately related to good interpersonal relations. Dudley Bennett suggests two of them: "People are not usually aware of how their behavior looks to others. Sometimes they wonder why they behave the way they do, but more often they wonder why others act as they do."[2] Knowing how you are preceived by others is the initial step in evaluating your impact on people, and feedback from other people is one of the most objective forms of information about you since there are really only two places feedback can come from: yourself and others. Each of us has an area of blindness regarding our interpersonal relationships. Without the help and feedback of others we can never fully understand how we relate and the effects of our relationships.[3]

Second, attempting to understand the strengths and weaknesses of others before you have confronted and accepted your own strengths and weaknesses will undermine your objectivity. Psychoanalysts call that *projection*. Third, whenever we talk about the virtues of self-awareness, we are making a value judgment. We are saying that it is better to be aware than unaware. We are convinced that that is true, but we also believe that there are many, many people who do not want to be self-aware.[4] Such persons are either very arrogant or they are stupid!

Getting the other person's point of view is important if we are to work together productively on committees. The importance of point of view is demonstrated in the discussion between Jesus and His disciples in Mark 8:27-9:1. Jesus was asking His followers who men thought He was. After receiving their replies, He proceeded to teach them that He must suffer many things, be killed and after three days rise again. At that point Peter rebuked Him for His statements. Jesus then turned to Peter and said, "Get behind Me, Satan, for you are not setting your mind on God's interests, but man's." In other words, Peter was rebuked because his outlook or point of view was faulty. That passage points out that God's point of view emphasized the Person of the Savior rather than self (Mark 8:34), the principle of giving rather than gaining (Mark 8:35) and the profits for eternity in contrast to the profits for time (Mark 8:36-38). It is clear, therefore, that one's point of view is very important. Peter could not understand the Person and the work of Christ without recognizing His point of view. When dealing with people, we should try to discover why they do what they do.

Someone has said, "To know all is to forgive all."[5] We will find it very difficult to understand people if we fail to be open-minded when we first meet them. There is a danger of prejudging a person because of dress, hair, etc. Such a prejudgment will tend to give a distorted impression of the individual because of our bias rather than on the basis of who the individual is.

If you want to evaluate a person, do you consider what they do or what they say? The answer is both, but if one must take precedence, which would you choose? Behavior, of course. If people say one thing and do something else, we have to believe what they do and not what they say. That is the message of cognitive dissonance. It is easier to rationalize our behavior than it is to change it.[6]

If we are to truly understand people, we must give consideration to their friendships. It has been said through the years that people are known by their friends.

We need to take time to observe a person's life if we are to come to a point of real understanding. We should take the time to visit the individual's home so that we can note the types of activities in various contexts.

It would be helpful to observe an individual's reaction in problem situations. This will give an indication of the ability or inability to handle stress. In the attempt to understand people a word of warning needs to be given. Beware of making yourself a psychiatrist when you are not one. There are two words of Scripture that contain the central truth of volumes of psychology books on the technique of working with people. In Matthew 7:1 we find the words, "Judge not." If Christian workers would abide by that scriptural admonition, they would have already taken the first step in understanding people.[7]

Relating to Others

If the revitalization process is to be effectively carried out, people must be able to relate to others.

Our present way of life develops what might be identified as a push-button technique. We walk into a room, flip the switch, and expect the light to go on. We step into a car, turn the ignition key, and expect the motor to turn over. There is a tendency to carry the same general approach over into the realm of dealing with people and expect that when we say, "Jump," they will automatically ask, "How high?" We forget that people can be recalcitrant. They have minds of their own and do not like to be pushed around. It is nice to be important, but it is more important to be nice.

Donald Sanzotta emphasizes several points worth remembering when striving to improve our relationship to others.[8] As we are working in small groups seeking to come to a consensus about goals, finances, and programs, we should strive to actually listen to what others in the group are saying. We cannot evaluate another's position unless we have given a careful hearing to it. It is unwise to try to change people; that is God's work. We should put our emphasis upon changing procedures. We should be willing to ask others for help when we need it. The process of sharing in the various aspects of the revitalization process is important. We should be willing to open our lives enough to let people know if we are hurting, what we hope, and how we actually feel.

No one in a leadership position can do too much listening. It has been said that the average manager spends up to 70 percent of his time listening. God gave us two ears and only one mouth. Someone has suggested that we should take a hint from that and listen twice as much as we talk. Someone asked Albert Einstein for the secret to success. He replied that the secret to success was threefold: it involves hard work, play, and the ability to keep the mouth shut.

Throughout the entire process of revitalization it is important that everyone have an opportunity to give input. Some of the suggestions may seem strange. Others will be in opposition to your own ideas. When such are offered, it is unwise to let one's temperament get out of control. There are many temperamental people in the world. Someone has suggested that the meaning of the term "temperamental" involves 90 percent temper and 10 percent mental instability. A person who is in a position of leadership and who is subject to moods and temper tantrums produces great turmoil and certainly will delay the revitalization process.

The overuse of defense mechanisms is the single most significant inhibitor of open and harmonious interpersonal relations. The list of defense mechanisms is a long one. Here are just three:

> *Reaction formation.* This involves beliefs or actions that are the opposite of the way a person unconsciously feels. Unacceptable feelings are denied by overreacting to them: "I am not prejudiced; if anything, I bend over backwards . . ."
>
> *Repression.* This is unconsciously motivated forgetting. Through repression, unacceptable thoughts are blocked out: "I don't remember your ever saying anything about those quality standards."
>
> *Intellectualization.* This means removing the emotional impact of an idea or behavior and substituting abstract verbiage.[9]

Why do defense mechanisms exist in the first place? The most widely accepted theory is that the defenses accomplish two purposes: they distort reality slightly, making circumstances and perceptions easier to accept emotionally, and they preserve or enhance self-esteem.[10]

In relating to people it is important that we possess and share joy, and that we be pleasant. Some Christians have seemingly felt that sanctification and sadness must go together. They feel that the more sanctified and holy the individual is, the more somber he or she will appear. That type of thinking has prompted one person to say that it would appear that some saints have been baptized in lemon juice. William James of Harvard stressed in his writings in psychology that action and feeling go together.[11] If that is true, let it be noted that we will feel better physically if we take the time and trouble to smile.

We should take the initiative to be friendly. It has been said that we should especially be friendly and kind to the people we meet on the way up the ladder of success, because it may be that we will meet them again on the way down. Do not try to discover whether people are friendly by waiting for them to speak to you. Rather, take the initiative to start a friendly conversation with them. When we speak of others, we should do so in a positive fashion. It was Benjamin Franklin who said, "I will speak ill of no man . . . and speak all the good I know of everybody."[12]

Knowing how to converse with people is important if we desire to get along with them. It is not always what we say, but how we say it that counts. The Lord Jesus was a master at conversation. The Scripture says that He spoke the truth in love (Eph. 4:15). He had the ability to contend for the faith without being contentious. His speech was always seasoned with grace. In Nazareth, "All were speaking well of Him, and wondering at the gracious words which were falling from His lips" (Luke 4:22). "In spite of his tone of authority and his fearless and scathing attacks on the times, there was diffused over all he said a glow of grace and love."[13]

When speaking with another person, we should not assume that the way we use a word is the same as the way the other individual uses that word. Language changes in the course of the years. Different sections of the country attach different meanings to different words and phrases. It is therefore imperative that we check on the connotative meaning of important words and phrases. In conversing with another do not contradict that individual until you are sure that you know exactly what the individual said.[14]

This sign was noted behind the registration desk at a conference. It conveyed a worthwhile message for those who would improve their conversational quality:

The six most important words—"I admit I made a mistake."
The five most important words—"You did a good job."
The four most important words—"What is your opinion?"
The three most important words—"If you please."
The two most important words—"Thank you."
The least important word—"I."

In talking with people it is wise to avoid arguments whenever possible. Really, the only way to get the best of an argument is to avoid it. It was Abraham Lincoln who is reported to have said, "A drop of honey catches more flies than a gallon of gall."[15] In matter of controversy some have a tendency to say, "My attitude is fine. I always see two points of view: the one that is wrong and mine."

Working Together

Working together will often demand reciprocal concessions. Where such concessions are not injurious to people or contrary to the gospel, they should be practiced. We recognize that when a weak or insincere man attempts to be all things to all men, he often ends up being nothing to anyone. We are not advocating such a procedure, but we are encouraging one to win for himself the esteem and love of those with whom he is dealing. We should be willing to be flexible.

There are times when negative feelings arise as we meet or work with individuals. We may have a tendency to "get a load off our chest" and thereby make public our negative feelings. We falsely think that we are punishing the other person by so doing. The truth of the matter is that by broadcasting our negative attitudes, we are bringing negative reflections upon ourselves. The reason for our negative feelings may be in us rather than in the other individual. One of the most basic and most overlooked ways of getting along with people is the use of *catharsis*. Therapeutically, the term implies the beneficial effect of expressing oneself. In emotional catharsis a person feels relief after talking out a problem.[16]

We should seek for the guidance of the Holy Spirit that we may discover the real source of the negative feelings and seek

His power to love the individual rather than to loathe him.

In order to please God and work well with His people we must avoid gossiping. In Proverbs 17:9 we read, "He who repeats a matter separates intimate friends." It is important that in counseling and caring we not reveal to outsiders that which transpires between individuals in confidence.

No one who aspires to work well with people can afford to ignore courtesy. Courtesy means being considerate of other in little things. It is one of the easiest qualities to lift one above the general life of the crowd. Courtesy and etiquette are closely connected. True etiquette, hospitality, courtesy, and good manners come from the heart. John Wesley used to say to his lay preachers, "Act as if you were brought up in court." The purpose of etiquette is to glorify God and become an effective witness.

The pattern of etiquette is to be found in the Lord Jesus. And the root of etiquette is established in 1 Corinthians 13. It can be powerfully stated in one word, *love*. In 1951 twenty-four leaders of the China Inland Missision Overseas Mission Fellowship gathered at Manila. They had left China and now had no specific leading as to the direction for the future. The last surviving daughter of General Booth came to speak at the conference. Her challenge was in the form of a question, "Gentlemen, how do you spell love?" She answered her rhetorical question with the word "sacrifice." Through that challenge, missions was reborn in Southeast Asia.

The quality of our relationships is the measure of our Christian authenticity. Relatability to groups as well as to other individuals is one of the keys to developing the revitalization process. The group activities highlighted in the earlier chapters of this book must be carried along by satisfactory relationships or they will not by any means produce their intended results.

To understand the behavior of persons in groups we must first look at the kinds of needs they have. Every person has three needs that power his behavior—the needs for inclusion, for control, and for affection.[17]

Inclusion means being able to take an interest in people and have people take an interest in us. It is the capacity for being accepted as part of a group. The inclusion phase in group behavior begins with the formation of the group. When people are first confronted with each other, they need to find out where they fit. Of the three inclusion types, the *undersocial* tends to be introverted and withdrawn. He avoids associating with others or taking part in group discussions and protects his privacy. The *oversocial* cannot stand being alone and therefore seeks people constantly. This person seems intensely interested in everything that is said in a group and must be involved in every topic that is raised. The *social* type enters relationships with interest in people and welcomes their interest. He offers acceptance and claims inclusion himself.

After the problems of inclusion have been somewhat resolved, the group enters the *control* phase. Control problems become prominent, and the issue arises as to who shall control their solutions. Characteristic behavior of this stage includes leadership struggles, competition, how the group shall be structured, and rules of procedure.

Control means having others respect and listen to you. Three types may be identified here also. The *abdicrat* tends toward submission to anyone and refuses all power and responsibility, thus forcing others to make decisions. The *autocrat*, on the other hand, tries to dominate at all times. The *democrat* seeks mutuality and fair distribution of authority and responsibility.

There is also the *affection* phase. This involves being able to relate to others with love and warmth. The first of three affection types is the *underpersonal*. That individual tends to avoid close personal ties with anyone and is most comfortable in relations that are impersonal and superficial. The *overpersonal*, on the other hand, wants to be extremely close to all people at all times. The *personal* type would fit between the underpersonal and overpersonal types. That type can participate in a group without dominating it. When the affection phase is considered in relation to group activity, the primary anxiety is the matter of being liked or not liked.

Unless the individuals within a group can relate satisfactorily to one another, the revitalization process will be hampered. Throughout all phases the question of compatibility is present. By compatibility, we mean a relationship that leads to mutual satisfaction of interpersonal needs. Inclusion incompatibility involves a conflict between those who prefer to work in teams and those who work best alone. Control incompatibility is evidenced when two people who both have a strong need to dominate are challenged to work together. In such a case too many leaders will produce group conflict. Affection incompatibility will take place when a person who needs warm, friendly relations with others is placed in a group of people who do not have a similar need.

The effects of incompatibility on a group's task performance is clear. The more compatible a group, the greater its chance of reaching its goals. The less compatibility among members, the more time the group must spend in dealing with interpersonal difficulties. That can delay the progression through the steps in the revitalization process.

LEARNING TO LEAD

If one is to be a leader of people, it is especially important that one knows how to get along with them. Our society encourages self-centeredness; we are told to "watch out for number one." That self-centeredness manifests itself in a lack of involvement in helping one another and in the manipulation of others for our own selfish ends.[18] Alfred Adler, the famous psychologist, states in his book *What Life Should Mean to You*, "It is the individual who is not interested in his fellow man who has the greatest difficulties in life and provides the greatest injury to others. It is from among such individuals that all human failure springs."[19]

The most significant indication to the understanding of a person is to find out what basically motivates his life.[20] It is important that the leader recognize that a person's salary is not a source of performance motivation. It has been stated that traditional rewards and incentives have little motivational effect on performance. It appears that work enrichment is far more meaningful. This involves such matters as making the work more challenging, more interesting, and more satisfying to the one who performs it. Effective performance is also enhanced as the individual sees the opportunity to achieve meaningful goals. The implications of this truth for working with people in the church are many. As one leads people, it is beneficial to let them share in decision-making, have more responsibility in the areas of planning and policymaking and to exert some influence in the area of spending money.

People develop best when they are deliberately given situations in which they can make their own choices, where they understand the context, and where their ideas contribute to results. They appreciate being permitted to experiment and share ideas without being subject to judgment. Mistakes need not be used as invitations to censure, punish, or judge. They may be used to provide new data about what not to do in the future.[21]

The leader of people should not change his chair into a throne. Only little people try to dominate rather than to inspire. Wise leaders use good will rather than fear. They do not strive to win their point by fighting but rather by having the people want to get behind their plans. Dr. Wendell White gives the following four suggestions for presenting one's ideas indirectly: 1) spare another from feeling inferior; 2) share another's feelings of independence; 3) afford another the satisfaction of having more or less originated the idea; and 4) help another not fear that unless he adheres to the idea, he will lose prestige.[22]

Leaders need to loosen the strings of control and allow greater freedom and responsibility within the work cycle. In our churches we are working with a "new breed" of laity. They have developed an ability and desire to share in the change process. It is for that reason we have emphasized revitalization as being a shared process between clergy and laity. Authority, however, needs to be coupled with responsibility. Prime Minister Churchill told the House of Commons on July 2, 1942, "I am your servant and you have the right to dismiss me when you please. What you have no right to do is ask me to bear responsibilities without the power of effective action."

One of our teaching colleagues said: "I would rather be a king-maker than to be a king." That has far-reaching, professional implications. If one is to be a successful leader, one needs to develop a reputation as being a helper of others. He must be able to work with people. The following list sets forth some practical suggestions in the area of leadership:

1. It is important to make clear and logical assignments of responsibilities. Those responsibilities should not duplicate the work of others, and it should be evident that they contribute to the total program.

2. Before a leader makes changes, the persons most affected by those changes should be involved in deciding what the changes will be.

3. It is important that the leader express confidence in the person's ability to do the work. He should praise every improvement.

4. The wise leader will seek to guide by stimulating thinking rather than by dictating action. This will involve planting seed thoughts, making suggestions, and asking questions rather than giving orders.

5. People should be helped to realize that others are depending on them.

6. A job description should be provided for each position. Helpers should not be enlisted unless they are needed.

It is important that one who is leading others be genuine, enthusiastic and sincere. The leader must be willing to admit his own mistakes. If a leader expects to see the development of strengths within those being led, he must be willing to put up with weaknesses. Individuals must be given an opportunity to grow and develop.

Maturing as Individuals

Growing up is a difficult discipline. We have seen the difficulty in others and after sober reflection remember that we did not have an easy time of it either. To mature is to come to completeness of growth and development. Childhood fades, adolescence advances, and adulthood arrives. We recognize the importance of physical maturity but sometimes overlook the importance of psychological and spiritual maturity. Dr. David MacLennan has said, "Spiritually mature persons alone can solve the problems of our time." Abigail VanBuren has said, "This is maturity: to be able to stick with a job until it is finished; to be able to bear injustice without wanting to get even; to be able to carry money without spending it; and to do one's duty without being supervised."

An individual who is spiritually mature is willing to accept and recognize his own imperfections (Phil. 3:12-16). Paul recognized that he had not already arrived nor was he already perfect, but he was pressing on through concentration and perseverance. We need to profit from our mistakes and shortcomings rather than to ponder over them.

An individual who is spiritually mature is willing to adopt a long-range scale of values (Phil. 3:7-11). Paul was willing to deny now in order to gain later (3:7). Adoniram Judson labored on the mission field for seven years before being privileged to see his first convert come to Christ. God does not settle all of His accounts every Saturday night, but He does settle all of His accounts in good time. We should be willing to work today and to be paid in God's tomorrow.

An individual who is spiritually mature is willing to adopt new ideas (1 Cor. 3:11). When one refuses to make new associations and develop new activities, one's life becomes limited and growth is stifled. Too often we have a tendency to say, "Come weal or come woe, my status is quo." An individual who is spiritually mature is one who acts in love (Eph. 4:15). That type of individual gets more satisfaction from giving than from receiving. He has the ability to control his feelings of hostility. He realizes that if he is going to love God, he must also love his brother (1 John 4:21).

Some words that are easiest to spell are most difficult to define. Three of those are one syllable words: *life, light,* and *love.* In the Greek language there are at least four ways of defining love. *Eros* refers to love between the sexes. It pertains to passion and sexual desire. This word is not in the New Testament. A second word refers to friendship or love for mankind. A third word involves love for a friend.

The fourth word is *agape.* That involves more than emotion. It involves the whole man and is used of man's love for God and God's love for man. It appears 120 times in the New Testament. "But earnestly desire the greater gifts. And I show you a still more excellent way. If I speak with the tongues of men and of angels, but do not have love, I have become a noisy gong or a clanging cymbol" (1 Cor. 12:31; 13:1).

We need faith, hope, and love, but love is superior. God's endowment of gifts to His people is the theme of 1 Corinthians 12. God's instruction for the use of those gifts is the theme of 1 Corinthians 14. The hymn of love in 1 Corinthians 13 provides God's energy to use those gifts to His glory.

Love makes actions profitable for time and eternity. Without it, profession is but pretense and service is fruitless. Love is sovereign in the heart. It must also be sovereign in the mind. It will provide power to declare the things of God, to discern spiritual things, and the intelligence to comprehend the truth. Love sanctifies every gift. Without it, I produce nothing of value, am of no value, and gain nothing of value. The value of love gives it the place of preeminence (1 Cor. 13:1-3).

Love develops Christian character in us (1 Cor. 13:4-7). "Love is patient, love is kind, and is not jealous; love does not brag" (1 Cor. 13:4). This was Queen Victoria's favorite verse. Love is difficult to define but is not difficult to discern. It does not retaliate, is kind, generous, and not puffed up. It makes no parade, is not rude, and seeks not its own. Love is not easily provoked, does not think evil, and is gladdened by goodness. Love bears and believes all things. It hopes and endures all things. Those first seven verses show the effect of love upon the individual.

Love provides an assurance of victory (1 Cor. 13:8-13). Prophecy may be made useless, and ecstatic utterances cease. Knowledge may pass away like the usefulness of an old encyclopedia, but love never fails (1 Cor. 13:8).

We are sons and daughters of God, and we know that when Christ comes again that we shall be like Him for we shall then see Him as He is (1 John 3:1-3). It will be then that our search for maturity will be complete. Until that day, we keep on striving. There is a marker over the resting place of one of the Alpine climbers, "He died climbing." It is hoped that that type of phrase can also be used for us as being indicative of our continual striving for spiritual maturity and proficiency in getting along with people.

In any revitalization process it is imperative that the leaders lead in such a way that the people are "brought willingly along." The people must feel included, respected, and "heard" or they will not support the process. Remember, people tend to support what they have helped to create.

To be successful in ministry it is necessary that you know how to get along with people. If you are having difficulty in this area of your life, we urge you to engage in some serious study in interpersonal relationships. Read some books; take some courses to improve your communication skills. The parish revitalization process, the ministry of the church, and you as a person will be much better because of it.

NOTES

1. Dale Carnegie, *How to Win Friends and Influence People* (New York: Simon and Schuster, Pocket, 1937), p. 3.
2. Dudley Bennett, *T. A. and The Manager* (New York: Amacom, 1976), p. 1.
3. Joseph Luft, *Group Processes: An Introduction to Group Dynamics* (Palo Alto, Calif.: National, 1970). For a most helpful discussion of our "blind spots" in relationships see his comments on the "Johari Window," pp. 11-20.
4. Donald Sanzotta, *The Manager's Guide to Interpersonal Relations* (New York: Amacom, 1979), p. 16.
5. Carnegie, p. 42.
6. Sanzotta, p. 104.
7. Donald Bell, *How to Get Along with People in the Church* (Grand Rapids: Zondervan, 1970), p. 57.
8. Sanzotta, pp. 102-131.
9. Ibid., p. 48.
10. Ibid., p. 49.
11. Carnegie, p. 101.
12. Ibid., p. 41.
13. James Stalker, *The Life of Christ* (New York: Revell, 1891), p. 71.
14. Dr. Thomas Gordon calls the process of being sure you understand the meaning behind another's words "active listening." For help in developing that skill, read Gordon's *Leadership Effectiveness Training* (New York: Wyden, 1977).
15. Carnegie, p. 182.
16. Sanzotta, p. 116.
17. William Schutz, *Interpersonal Underworld* (Palo Alto, Calif.: Science and Behavior Books, 1966). Schutz discusses the needs of people who make up a group.
18. Gary Collins, *Living in Peace* (Wheaton, Ill.: Key, 1970), pp. 24-35.
19. Carnegie, p. 85.

20. Bell, p. 64.
21. Jut Meininger, *Success Through Transactional Analysis* (New York: New American Library, Signet, 1973), p. 206.
22. Wendell White, *The Psychology of Dealing with People* (New York: Macmillan, 1936), pp. 3-7.

7

Missional Aspects of Revitalization

A church that has been singing as a "theme song" at every service for a century, "as it was in the beginning is now and every shall be, world without end, Amen" will find it difficult to get out of the traditional ditch by the side of the road and get onto the highway for God. There may be some strong opposition to revitalization because it will mean change.

In a chapter every church leader should read, Peter Drucker declares, "All service institutions (churches included) are threatened by the tendencies to cling to yesterday rather than to slough it off, and put their best and ablest people on defending what no longer makes sense or serves a purpose."[1] He goes on to say the rule of most service institutions is "whatever we do, we'll do forever," whereas the proper rule is "whatever we do today will in all likelihood be a candidate for abandonment within a fairly short period of years."

Paul the apostle was not content with mediocrity. "Not that I have already obtained it, or have already become perfect, but I press on in order that I may lay hold of that for which also I was laid hold of by Christ Jesus. Brethren, I do not regard myself as having laid hold of it yet; but one thing I do: forgetting what lies behind and reaching forward to what lies ahead, I press on toward the goal for the prize of the upward call of God in Christ Jesus" (Phil. 3:12-14).

Revitalization depends partly upon the inflow of new ideas and new programs that will capture the interest and imagination of the people. Many saints of God have served faithfully and well but are now getting tired. They sense that the end of the road may be getting close. They are now dreaming of a different and better land. But "until then" we must do our best for the glory of the Lord in the here and now. In many churches revitalization will have to be pursued by new people who have not become stuck in the ruts of mediocrity. The new program will have to be advanced by those new members who have not become saturated with traditional, habitual practices.

Reaching new people is an essential element of the revitalization process. There are plenty of people to be reached. The question is, What process can we use to reach the people so that they can become involved in the revitalization process of the church?

Two and one-half billion of the world's 4.5 billion population have never had an adequate witness of God's plan of salvation through Jesus Christ.[2] In the midst of the evangelical surge revealed by a recent Gallop Poll, 41 percent of all Americans over eighteen, or 61 million, are still functionally unchurched.[3]

Around 1960 some changes took place in American life that in turn brought about changes in church membership. It may have been that the increase of wealth pulled people away from the church. It may have been that they were too busy to find time for church. There may have been disturbing events in public life that detracted from church. Disturbances in the area of social action had an impact upon church participation. As the median age of the membership changes, the mainline church is confronted especially with the task of attracting and holding young people. It has not shown itself very adept at that in recent years.

Membership decline among the denominations that stand in the Reformation tradition has been upsetting. Those mainline denominations include the Congregational, Episcopal, Methodist, Lutheran, Presbyterian, and Reformed. The United Methodist church membership declined by more than one million in the past decade. The United Presbyterian and Episcopal churches show losses of more than half a million members each. The Lutheran Church in America is off by a quarter of a million.

Dr. Charles Chaney of the Southern Baptist Convention reminds us that there are four types of growth. The first type is internal and involves edification and the growth in grace. The second is expansion growth. That is numerical and involves an increase in the local congregation. The third type of growth is extension, which occurs when a sponsoring church starts a work in a neighboring community. The fourth type of growth takes place when a sponsoring church starts a work across a significant cultural barrier.

Outreach into communities for more church support should not begin with a plan or program but with a clear sense of purpose. That sense of purpose must be acknowledged by the organizers and those who are to participate. It is imperative that we know why we are doing what we are doing. Many church programs have collapsed because purpose orientation has been neglected. In chapter 1 purpose orientation is referred to as mission clarification.

Several questions, when answered, will provide some clarification of purpose for outreach into the community.

1. Why should the church reach out to the community?
2. Why should the community be interested in the church?
3. What are some hindrances to church outreach?
4. What qualities should one possess as equipment for reaching out?
5. Where are some places we should go in order to reach individuals?
6. Where and with whom should we start the outreach program?
7. What agencies outside the church can help us in the outreach program?
8. What are the limits of the members' responsibility for reaching out?

As archaeologists dig back into those early cities, they find no church foundations before A.D. 160. That means for the first 120 years Christians met exclusively in houses, and that was a great advantage to the church. A "church" was not a congregation of 5,000 or 2,000 or even 200. A church was an assemblage of fifteen to twenty people, or at the most thirty people. Everybody knew everybody else; they cared for everybody else. It was a household of God.

Scriptures were used by the early church as the divine instrument provided by the Holy Spirit for evangelism. Chirgwin calls the Bible an "indispensable tool" in the expansion of the early church: "It seems beyond dispute that the early Christian preachers and writers constantly used the Scriptures as a means of persuading non-Christians to accept the faith. The Bible was the regular tool of their evangelism."[4] Eusebius (A.D. 260-340) recorded how the postapostolic believers inspired "by the holy word" sacrificially went out to evangelize and committed to their converts "the books of the divine Gospels."[5]

Theology of Church Growth

New Testament churches grew in many different types of circumstances. That growth was seen in periods of great revival (Acts 2:41), in times of tension (Acts 4), in civil peace (Acts 9), as a consequence of spontaneous witnessing (Acts 11:19), and as a consequence of organized planned teaching (Acts 11:22-24; 12:48).

The growth of churches is related intimately and primarily to the proclamation of the Scriptures. For that reason Paul exhorts Timothy to "preach the Word" (2 Tim. 4:2), for the Bible is living and active (Heb. 4:12). The Bible is God's appointed instrument and means for the salvation and sanctification of men. The power for church growth does not lie only in the *nature* of the truth contained in the Scriptures even though there is more moral power in the doctrine of God alone "than in all the systems of moral philosophy."[6] The disciplines of sociology, anthropology, communication, and psychology, although helpful to understand the growth of the churches, do not possess the power to make them grow.

In Acts 1:8 we read, "But you shall receive power when the Holy Spirit has come upon you; and you shall be My witnesses both in Jerusalem, and in all Judea and Samaria, and even to the remotest part of the earth." That is the commission of the Christian. After Jesus had said that, He was taken up while they were watching, and a cloud swept under Him and carried Him out of their sight.

Jesus went up. The Holy Spirit came down. The disciples went out. Those disciples were lowly men with no special talents. Their hopes had been dashed to pieces at the cross, but fifty days later on Pentecost they received a new power, became aware of their purpose, and were given a plan.

The Holy Spirit is a "helper" who can be invoked, grieved, or resisted by the believer. Therefore, the walk of the witness influences the effectiveness of his ministry.

Although the Reformation brought a renewal of church life and theology, it was Philip Jacob Spener who ignited the sparks of revival amid dead orthodoxy by teaching the centrality of Scripture, the return of Christ, and the necessity of Jewish evangelism. Renewed attention was given to the personal faith and holiness of life based upon the ministry of the Holy Spirit and the Scriptures.[7]

We have biblical grounds substantiating the fact that a church should and can grow. Growth is the work and will of God (1 Cor. 3:5-7). Growth is an innate quality of the New Testament church (Eph. 2:20-22). It is the very nature of the gospel (Col. 1:3-3). A study of the churches of the New Testament gives evidence of the fact that those churches grew in all types of circumstances.

Acts 2:41	In periods of great revival
Acts 4	In times of tension
Acts 5:14; 6:1, 7	In times of inner church tension
Acts 9	In civil peace
Acts 11:9-21, 19	As a consequence of spontaneous witnessing
Acts 11:22-24; 12:48	As a consequence of organized, planned teaching
Acts 16:5	As they expounded apostolic injunctions of Acts 15
Acts 19:10-20	As a result of planned efforts (cf. Colossian church)

Since God has assigned the highest priority to bringing men into a living relationship to Jesus Christ, we can define mission narrowly as an enterprise devoted to proclaiming the good news of Jesus Christ and to persuading men to become His disciples and dependable members of His church.

Need for Church Growth

There are many reasons for the lack of growth within the

organized church. One of those is found in spiritual problems that hinder growth. Much of the energy within the membership is wasted in struggling over divisions. Unconfessed sins hinder the working of the Holy Spirit. Held grudges stifle growth activity.

Another reason centers in the fact that church leaders are often tied to unproductive work. The first two chapters of this book should help to break that futile cycle. Only a very small part of their time is spent in reaching people. There is a tendency to address the message of the church to a limited portion of the population.

Many suffer from a no-growth myopia. They neither expect nor want the church to grow. They therefore have no plans for growth. The lack of lay involvement hampers church growth and expansion. There is a tendency to make the present organizations ends in themselves.

Four "easy" answers have been given in reply to the question, "Why isn't the church growing?" The first of those stresses the mobility of people. We are a society on wheels. It is true that people move out, but it is also true that newcomers arrive. A second easy answer says that, "When I preach the gospel, they don't come." On the other hand, many say that they preach the gospel and that is the reason for people coming. Others will answer that we are living in the last days, namely the Laodicean era. If that is a real cause for a church not growing, how does it happen that in the midst of such an era, some churches are growing very rapidly? The fourth easy answer is that the pastor and members of today's churches are not spiritual.

In contrast to those easy answers some hard ones may be advanced. Spiritual problems hinder church growth. Divisions have diffused and consumed growth energy. Unconfessed sins have hindered the working of the Spirit. Spiritual honesty opens the gate for growth. If the church is to grow, Christ must be in control. In some cases it appears that the congregation may have the same ethical standards as the world. Growth is stifled in the church because many of the leaders are tied to unproductive work.

A few evangelical denominations show membership increases. The Southern Baptists have two million more than they had a decade ago. The Seventh-Day Adventists have increased by 35 percent. The Church of the Nazarene has increased by 40 percent.

The emphasis on church growth presupposes that it is possible to get a church out of its holding pattern. The following suggestions may prove helpful.

Diagnose the church record. That diagnosis should cover the past ten years of church activity. What has been the yearly rate of growth? How have members been added to the church? Has the church been losing members? Where did the new members come from? What kind of leadership does the church have?

A second step to take would be to get to know the unchurched members of the community. Find out the cultural, racial, social, and economic situation.

A third step involves clarifying a dream that will stretch your faith. The whole revitalization process set forth in the first four chapters of the book should do this. Those dreams should be turned into goals and announced publicly. The people should be challenged to make a commitment toward having a share in bringing those goals to pass.

A fourth step involves mobilizing the membership for growth. New Christians should be challenged at once to become involved in evangelism. The membership should be challenged to become involved in effective prayer and Bible study. A prayerful attempt should be made to create an atmosphere in which the membership will expect growth.

The final suggestion involves discovering and using methods that have proved effective in today's society, not those that worked a decade or a generation ago. When those methods have been uncovered, they should be evaluated in light of the character and life-style of the church and community. Be sure that at each step you seek the leading of the Spirit of God.

NOTES

1. Peter Drucker, *Management* (New York: Harper & Row, 1973), p. 146.
2. Ralph D. Winter, *Penetrating the Last Frontiers* (Pasadena, Calif.: US Center for World Mission, 1978).

3. "Gallop Poll: An Overview of Christianity Today," *Christianity Today*, 21 December 1979.
4. A. M. Chirgwin, *The Bible in World Evangelism* (New York: Friendship, 1954), p. 21.
5. Stephen Neill, *A History of Christian Missions* (Baltimore: Penguin, 1964), p. 40.
6. Charles Hodge, *Systematic Theology III* (Grand Rapids: Eerdmans, 1946), p. 471.
7. Phillip Jacob Spener, *Theologische Bedencken* (Halle: Verlegung des Waysen-Houses, 1700), pp. 159-62. A broader definition of mission would add to the proclaiming of the good news of Jesus Christ the development of an organization unit that would strengthen and spread that witness.

8

Proclamational Aspects of Revitalization

There have been three stages of church renewal literature. From 1950 to 1962 the emphasis was upon criticizing the church. The literature was analytical and critical. From 1962 to 1967 there was a great emphasis placed upon the nature and the mission of the church. The literature was theoretical and theological. Beginning in 1967 there was a change of emphasis in that more time and space was given to providing some practical assistance and positive suggestions for improvement.[1]

We believe that church renewal or church revitalization is primarily the work of God. He performs that work through men and women who make up His church. That process will involve the rediscovery of purpose, a reawakening of a sense of mission, a redefinition of goals, and a renewing of the spirit of the membership.[2]

One of the most effective means of preparing a church for an experience of revitalization is through biblical preaching, which makes a clear connection between what the Bible says and the processes the church is using to clarify mission and establish goals. Biblical preaching can help the membership of the church see the biblical foundations for their purposes and activities.

It was Phillips Brooks who emphasized in his Beecher lectures on preaching that preaching was one of the best means of communicating God's truth to persons through a person. He declared his confidence in God's power to change persons through the preaching of God's good news. The neglect of biblical preaching weakens the witness of the church because it violates the biblical image of the ministry.

It was through preaching that the church was planted in a pagan world. It was through preaching that the church was renewed in the sixteenth century. It was through preaching that the dreadful social conditions were corrected in eighteenth century England. One important factor in our modern crusade for revitalization in the twentieth century church is biblical preaching. Preaching alone is not enough to sustain revitalization over a long period, but it is a critical element of any revitalization effort. If preaching alone were enough, every church would be revitalized since preaching is the main activity of most evangelical pastors.

We realize that positive support for biblical preaching as an important factor in church revitalization is not warmly received in many pious secular communities. There is a tendency to respect Jesus but not to become vitally involved with Him. There is a tendency to venerate the Bible but not to really study it to discern God's methods for making men good and His church effective. There is a tendency to make sure that there is a church for baptizing, marrying, and burying, but not to regard it as the body of believers who are committed to Jesus Christ.

There is a need for a biblical approach to church revitalization. This biblical approach can be conveyed to the people of God through biblical preaching and Bible study. The Bible contains the principles necessary for lasting spiritual church revitalization.

We would encourage church theologians to formulate a theology for church revitalization. How has God worked in and through His people through the years? This theology for revitalization can then become content for the preaching ministry. There needs to be a correlation between biblical principles and present day cultural realities.

In the next few pages we have sought to provide some material which may prove homiletically suggestive for Bible messages conveying some of the basic concepts of church revitalization. The areas covered in this section are dealt with and developed in the earlier chapters of this book. The biblical foundations are developed from a study of God's Word.

We warn preachers who may read this section to beware of

the practice of prooftexting. Such a practice involves getting an idea from outside the Bible and then searching for a text of Scripture to attach to it. It is our conviction that that is not true biblical preaching. We feel that the ideas should arise from the study of the Scripture and that those ideas when directed and developed through the ministry of the Holy Spirit will result in practical application. We encourage the preacher to use larger passages as bases for his preaching. That will help him avoid the temptation of preaching upon a text without a context and thereby arriving at a pretext. The setting of the text should be recognized and developed.

Two books will be especially helpful in the process of constructing biblical messages relevant to the demands of today's church situation: *Biblical Preaching for Today's World* and *Expository Preaching Without Notes*.[3] These books emphasize the necessity of having a sermon methodology. They recognize that an expository sermon involves exposition plus application. They deal with the science of sermon construction rather than with the art of sermon presentation.

REVITALIZATION IN THE OLD TESTAMENT

A careful study of the five periods of reformation in the books of Chronicles and Kings will provide some clarification of God's method of revitalizing His people in Old Testament days. Some hints may be gleaned from a study of these passages that will provide ideas as to possible methods God may use with His people in our day.

In 2 Chronicles 15:8-19 and 1 Kings 15:9-24 there was an emphasis upon the need for repentance if God was to work constructively among His people. His people needed to depart from sin and turn to God. Scripture emphasizes that repentance is a timeless factor that is necessary if we are to have God's blessing. "The LORD is with you when you are with Him. And if you seek Him, He will let you find Him; but if you forsake Him, He will forsake you" (2 Chron. 15:2). Repentance, however, is just the point of beginning. If that were all that was needed, many evangelical churches would have been revitalized a thousand times, for they have heard the call to repentance constantly. There is a positive and constructive work which must follow repentance.

In 2 Chronicles 20 and 1 Kings 22:2-30 the emphasis is upon the necessity for prayer. These passages include Jehoshaphat's prayer in which he emphasizes God's almighty power and faithfulness. The prayer also emphasizes the comparative helplessness of the people. That early reformation emphasized the importance of seeking God's help in the revitalization of His people. It is disastrous to try to plan God's work without seeking God's guidance. The rich fool in Luke 12 left God out of his planning and philosophy of life and lost everything that really counted. Prayer is a two-way communication system. We make our needs known to God and He makes His ways known to us. The priorities of any group will be evidenced in their planning and budgeting. A timeless truth in Matthew 6:33 should be recognized: When God's kingdom is put first, He has promised to supply the needs. In 2 Chronicles 20:15, God reminded Jehoshaphat that the battle was not his but God's. We are colaborers together with God (1 Cor. 3:9).

In 2 Chronicles 24 and 2 Kings 12 the emphasis is upon disobedience to God's directions. God had told His people to repair the breaches of the house of God. For twenty-three years they had failed to do as God had commanded them. Joash then determined to obey God's directive and gave attention to the condition of the house of God. The prayer of the second reformation had to be followed by the obedience of the third reformation. "If . . . My people who are called by My name humble themselves and pray, and seek My face and turn from their wicked ways, then I will hear from heaven, will forgive their sin, and will heal their land" (2 Chron. 7:14). The whole revitalization process must be carried out in obedience to God's directions.

In 2 Chronicles 29-32 and 2 Kings 18-20, which give the account of the fourth reformation, the emphasis is upon the need for worship. Hezekiah opened the doors of the house of the Lord and repaired them. The public worship of God was then restored. In worshiping God, we get to know Him. We agree with A. W. Tozer when he wrote, "If we would bring back spiritual power in our lives, we must think of God more nearly as He really is."[4] In our planning, mission clarification, and budgeting we can expand our vision since we have a great God with whom we are working.

In 2 Chronicles 34-35 and 2 Kings 22-23:30 we have the account of the fifth reformation. The emphasis on that occasion was upon the importance of God's Word. Most of the Old Testament renewals were stimulated by the reading and expounding of the Law (Deut. 11:18-25). The Bible includes the directions for carrying out God's work. It is the rule of faith and practice. God's purposes and plans for His work are included in His Word. We advocate that God's people formulate their plans and carry out those plans in accord with Scripture. It is important that the actions involved in revitalization not contradict the Word of God. Methods may change, but the basic principles remain the same.

The study of God's Word brought some interesting profits. Hilkiah said to Shaphan the scribe, "I have found the book of the law in the house of the LORD" (2 Chron. 34:15). That discovery of the Word and its message resulted in a broken spirit. There were tender, humble, and repentant hearts. Because of that broken-heartedness, the Lord heard their prayers (34:27). There was also the result of a concerned spirit (34:21). That concern was prompted by a sense of sin (34:25), which led to a manifestation of concern for others. The final profit gleaned from a study of the Word was that of an obedient spirit (34:31). There was a determination to walk after the Lord and to keep His commandments. Those profits were action-oriented. Cardijn says that the Christian imperative is to see, judge, and act. He goes on to say that to see means to take a look at the world around you so that you may see the needs. To judge is to decide what God would have you do about those needs in accordance with the Word of God. To act involves doing what you perceive to be the instructions in the Word. All of this seems to equal revitalization. The study of the Word thus prompts God's people to see, judge, and act.

PROCLAMATION OF THE NATURE OF THE CHRUCH

One of the primary sources of tension within the church is the failure of its members to have a common understanding of the nature and purpose of the church they desire to see revitalized.

The church does not really have the right to chart its own

course. The church belongs to Christ. It is His by production. It is His by possession and His for preservation (Matt. 16:13-20). The church is a spiritual organism and cannot fulfill its intended function apart from being Spirit-filled.

The church is a company of people divinely called and separated from the world who are united in worship and service under the supreme authority of Christ with His Word as their rule of faith and practice. The church is not a building for shelter, a lodge for fellowship, or an insurance agency where we pay our premiums twice a year in return for safety and coverage. A clarification of the nature and intended function of the church will help us evaluate its value and effectiveness. When we look at the church as a field, we preach only for repentance. When we look at the church as a force, we preach for action. It has been wisely stated that one of the best tests of preaching effectiveness is that which happens to the person in the pew. Planning, budgeting, and evaluating are all a part of the process of seeing, judging and acting. Preaching motivates the listeners to carry out those actions. Preaching also provides guidelines for the processes.

The epistle of Paul to the Ephesians has been identified as the epistle with a primary emphasis upon the church. It states that the church was constituted by the plan of God the Father through the process of election (Eph. 1:3-6). It was constituted by the provision of the Son in redemption (Eph. 1:7-12). The preservation of the church was in accordance with the pledge of the Spirit (Eph. 1:13-14).

The church was the most wonderful body ever formed. It was quickened by the grace of God, the Father (Eph. 2:1-10). It was formed by the blood of Christ, the Son (Eph. 2:11-17). We have access to the church through one Spirit (Eph. 2:18).

In chapter 3 of Ephesians two main purposes are given for the church. The first is to reveal the wisdom of God (Eph. 3:1-13). Another purpose of the church is to experience the fullness of God (Eph. 3:14-19). The purposes of a church are very important in that the definition of purpose should influence the actions and attitudes of every person in the congregation. The purposes should be evidenced in the budget. The purposes should be evidenced in the program. We begin with purpose and then proceed with planning, program and performance.

A careful study of the six analogies used in Ephesians in connection with the church will help us to understand its purposes. A series of messages preached upon those analogies will help the people in the congregation determine why they are involved in church work. In Ephesians 1:22-23 the church is set forth as being a body for service. There must be life in the body if it is to serve. In Ephesians 2:21-22 the church is referred to as being a temple for worship. This emphasizes the importance of keeping in contact with God. In Ephesians 3:15 the analogy of the family is used which emphasizes the purpose of fellowship. In Ephesians 4:11 a new word appears for the first time in the letter. We refer to the term *pastor-teacher*. Teachers are connected with schools; therefore, the inference can be drawn that the church should consider teaching as one of its purposes. The fifth chapter sets forth the church as being a bride. Manifesting love and affection should be one of the purposes of the church (Eph. 5:32). The last chapter of Ephesians in verses 10 through 20 points out the fact that the church is an army. As an army the church is to do warfare with Satan.

The church is not like a pile of sand consisting of a dead mass of similar particles, nor is it like a cage of wild animals with its participants tearing one another apart. The church is the Body of Christ (1 Cor. 12:27). G. Campbell Morgan stated that he felt that this was the most valuable chapter in the New Testament in its presentation of the nature and function of the church.

In 1 Corinthians 12:4-11 the form of the church is emphasized. There are nine gifts, which may be classified into three groups. They are abilities for service.[5] Edification appears to be the key to this passage in that each is given for the common good (1 Cor. 12:7). Each member of the Body has a specific function to perform. We have discussed some of those functions in the earlier chapters of this book. The functions of the Body of Christ are also set forth here in 1 Cor. 12:12-26. The process of managment in the church should blend those functions together. As in a body, so in the church, individualism and isolation should not characterize the functioning of the parts. Collective decision-making and group processes will tend to strengthen the church, which is His Body. "God has placed the members [organs], each one of them, in the body, just as He desired" (1 Cor. 12:18). It would be ridiculous for the hand to try to be isolated from the rest of the body or for the ear to be jealous of the other parts of the body (1 Cor. 12:14, 16).

A body would be a monstrosity if it had only one function. By God's own design each member has a specific function, a ministry that no one else can do. The church must facilitate each person's discovering and performing that ministry. We should not envy the function of others nor should we despise the function of others (1 Cor. 14-26). We should seek to discover our particular function within the body that is His church and develop that function to His glory. Preaching should encourage the members to determine and develop the particular function for which they have responsibility within the body. God gives the gifts but not all to all the people.

Proclamation Through Witnessing

Proclamation by means of a daily witness can further the process of revitalization. That witness is normally thought of as being only verbal. It is more than that—it is an action as well. It is a witness through words and works. The members should be challenged through the preaching ministry to develop such a witness. Biblical biographical preaching can provide guidance and motivation.

An example of characteristics that should be evident in the lives of church members and leaders is the life of Stephen. Stephen was a layman. We agree with Gabriel Fackre when he writes, "the function of the church to be the salt of the earth can only be fulfilled by the laity."[6] Unless the layman fulfills his function as a witness, there will be vast areas of our lives in which there will be no Christian witness.

The witness for Christ in the life of Stephen was evident in his countenance. His face shone like the face of an angel (Acts 6:15). Alfred Lord Tennyson in his poem *Two Voices* says:

> He heeded not reviling tones
> Nor sold his heart to idle moans
> Tho' cursed and scorned and bruised with stones
> But looking upward full of grace
> He prayed and from a happy place
> God's glory smote him on the face.[7]

The angelic glow comes from having a privileged position, perfect obedience, personal purity and perpetual fellowship with the Father.

Stephen proclaimed his relationship to Christ through his character (Acts 6:3). He had a good reputation among the brethren. Even when they cast him out of the city and stoned him, he prayed for their forgiveness (Acts 6:60). His conversation identified him as one of God's workers. In Acts 7:2-60 we have an account of his apology. The personal element is missing. There is no personal defense. It is rather a witness to the supremacy of the spiritual. The glory of God was the theme of his apology.

Even in the depth of his commitment there was a proclamation of that relationship to God and His cause (Acts 7:59-60). Stephen's death is the only recorded biblical death other than the death of Jesus which is set forth in such detail. The test of a full life is not what it consumes but what it accomplishes. It was the life and death of Stephen that opened the door for the Gentiles. The Lord was glorified both by his life and by his death.

The proclamational aspects of revitalization can be seen in the life of one such as Stephen or in the experience of a Spirit-filled church such as the one recorded in Acts 2:1-47. It was while the Day of Pentecost was being fulfilled that the company of believers were gathered in one place. They were obedient, expectant, prayerful, and united (Acts 2:1). There came a sound like a rushing wind and they were all filled with the Spirit (Acts 2:2-4). When the multitude saw what was happening to the people as a result of their being filled with the Spirit, they were astonished and bewildered (Acts 2:6). They were engaged in an enthusiastic, missionary-type ministry. The ministry of the church of our day must also bring evidence to those who observe it that God is at work in the midst of His people and in the world. The church must respond both to the imperatives of the Word and the pressing human needs around the community.

The message of that church was a Bible-centered, positive, and prayer-supported message. The resurrection of Christ was declared, predicted, attested, and proved (Acts 2:23-37). The message was presented with convicting power. When they heard it, they were constrained to do something about it.

The members of that Spirit-filled congregation met some rather clear qualifications. First of all, they had to repent and be baptized in the name of Jesus Christ unto the remission of sins. They then received the gift of the Holy Spirit for service (Acts 2:38). Revitalization of the church is in two phases. It involves first of all repentance and then service. Many evangelical churches emphasize the first but overlook the second. It is interesting to note the ministries in which that church was engaged (Acts 2:42). They were united and had everything in common (Acts 2:44). They sold and shared, ate with gladness and singleness of heart, and kept praising God (Acts 2:44-47). They continued to maintain a good reputation among all of the people.

REVITALIZATION AND CHURCH MINISTRIES

Christ was concerned that His church be characterized by revitalization. The messages to the seven churches delineated in Revelation 2-3 have been referred to as Christ's last message to His church. G. Campbell Morgan refers to those chapters as the first-century message to the twentieth century Christians.[8] A careful study of those seven churches will show us that the need of the church for revitalization is most clearly seen in Revelation 2-3.

At least three different interpretations can be used in studying those churches. We can use a contemporary approach and consider them direct messages to the churches of John's own day. We could take the chronological approach and see in those churches a panoramic history of the church from Pentecost to the Rapture. We prefer a composite approach which regards the letters to the churches as being applicable to the churches in all ages. We do not exclude the first two approaches, but prefer to use all three.

The need of the church for revitalization is seen in the fifty-one verses that comprise one-eighth of the book of Revelation. Two of the churches are good churches. Two of the churches are bad churches. Three of the churches could be designated as being both good and bad. Each of the messages to the seven churches provides guidelines toward revitalization. A series of messages on those seven churches will show your members pitfalls to avoid and steps to take toward bringing new vigor into Christ's church.

The message to the church at Sardis recorded in Revelation 3:1-6 emphasized the need for us to give evidence that the church is alive. The Lord of the lampstands sent a message to the church at Sardis and said, "You have a name that you are alive, but you are dead" (Rev. 3:1). How does one measure the life of a church? Is it measured by the number of committee meetings held, or the amount of promotion and publicity, or the number of clubs? Is it not possible for the church to be like a furnace whose blower may still be going even though the fire is out? They spoke of Sardis as being alive when actually there was not growth but retrogression, not compassion but coldness, not unity but disintegration, and not joy but sadness. They had a form but were no longer a force. Christ desired that the church live up to its reputation. He administered a rebuke, advised a remedy, and admonished them to strive for the rewards promised to the overcomers.

The rebuke pertained to the discrepancy between the reputation they stimulated from the outside and the life they were actually living on the inside. It was evidently socially distinguished but was actually a spiritual graveyard. They were carrying on the routine duties but were not fulfilling the purpose and plan of God (Rev. 3:2). With their lips they were honoring God, but their hearts were removed far from Him (Isa. 29:13). Their hypocrisy was no secret as far as God was concerned. The church of our day often gives evidence to the outside world of being a very vital organization. That impression may be given by its large buildings and socially elite membership. The real test comes when the spiritual life of the congregation is analyzed. Outside adornment does not always mean that there is life within. Is the church really reaching out to help those in need? Are there planning and purposeful activity? Someone has noted the main difference between a rut and a grave—one is deeper than the other.

The remedy to be applied in order to alleviate the disorder consisted of several admonitions (Rev. 3:2-3). They were to be awake, or in other words, become watchers. They were to strengthen that which remained and was good. Those were the elements of faith and works that were still there. They were to remember what they had received and what they had heard. They were to keep those things and to repent once and for all. Service was to follow that repentance. If that remedy was not applied, then the One who had the seven spirits of God would come to them in judgment as a thief comes at nighttime when not expected.

A splendid threefold reward was offered if the church at Sardis took the corrective measures. The overcomers would be arrayed in white garments that they might walk with the One who had the seven stars in His hands (Rev. 1:16; 3:1). Their saintly character and service would be evident to all. Their names were to be inscribed permanently in God's book of remembrance. The Lord of the lampstands finally promised to confess their name before the Father. That is the victor's recognition by his commanding officer, Jesus Christ. A revitalized church will bring blessing to the membership. It will provide a good testimony to the community. It will glorify Christ.

Sardis had substituted the outward for the inward. That had to be rectified. The Christ of the candlesticks challenges the church to "be for real." The reputation before man must be a reality before God or it is of little value. The rebuke for hypocrisy is sharp. The remedy is clear. The reward is precious.

The message to the church at Ephesus recorded in Revelation 2:1-7 tells us that we should remember the importance of having a heart-love for Christ. It was Hudson Tayler who said, "The requirement for a missionary is not love for souls, but for the Lord." That was the truth the church at Ephesus missed.

It was at Ephesus that Paul had met some of his strongest opposition. It was also in that same city that he had been able to do some of his greatest work. We learn from Paul's experience at Ephesus that opposition cannot thwart the work for God indefinitely. The temple of Diana at Ephesus was one of the seven wonders of the world. Its one-hundred columns, fifty-six feet high, and its thirty-six hand-carved doors loomed above the city that could be characterized as the Vanity Fair of Asia.

The church within this city was a privileged church. It was the only one of the seven with an extensive spiritual background (Acts 18-20). Among their wonderful people they listed Priscilla and Aquilla. Among their wonderful preachers they listed Apollos and Paul, who had preached there for three months. The church had witnessed wonderful works with the bonfire of books of black magic (Acts 19:19). They had seen the shocking experience of the sons of Sceva (Acts 19:13-16). They had seen Demetrius and the silversmiths. Thirty years after that, the privileged church was called to revival.

The church within the city was a productive church (Rev. 2:2-3). It was noted for good works, labor, patience, and the fact that it could not bear to have evil ones in its midst. They sifted their membership and evidently applied discipline. They even tried those who said they were apostles and thereby guarded their pulpit. They had endured for the sake of Christ and had not grown weary. The church had kept the Nicolaitans away who evidently in those days were those who promised liberty but practiced corruption. The church evidently had plenty of zeal and orthodoxy but had one fault. They had lost their first love. They did not love Christ now the way they had loved Him at the beginning of their experience with Him (Rev. 2:4). This church emphasizes the fact that there is more to church work than good works, labor, patience, and fighting against evil ones. There is the positive item of a heart love for Christ. This is why worship, preaching, Bible study, and other similar activities are important features in revitalization. The spiritual background of that church was in the past.

The church in Ephesus had great possibilities if it could recapture its first love for Christ. Without such, duties become burdens. Without such an experience, the attractiveness is marred. The motivation for service is missing. "We love Him because He first loved us" (1 John 4:19). This church already had work, labor, and patience as noted in the Thessalonian church (see 1 Thess. 1:3), but was missing the important faith, love, and hope (Rev. 2:2). The ardor and love for Christ could return, however, providing they were willing to follow the spiritual prescription (Rev. 2:5). They must first of all remember from whence they had fallen. They must repent. That meant turning around or having a change of heart and attitude. They must repeat the earlier works. Before they could feel the first feelings they must do the first works.

Disaster came to the church because of its refusal to accept the prescription for revival. We must not overlook the importance of the spiritual condition of the heart in this whole process of revitalization. Delight was promised for the overcomers. They would be privileged to eat of the tree of life, which is the paradise of God (Rev. 2:7).

The message to the church at Laodicea recorded in Revelation 3:14-20 warns the church to avoid the pitfalls which lead to disaster. Five of the seven churches are commended, but there is no commendation for Sardis and Laodicea. There were at least a few faithful still in Sardis. The church at Laodicea had gone from spiritual heights to spiritual depths. That group of worshipers had been the subject of Paul's prayers and tears (Col. 2). The son of Philemon is said to have been the pastor of the church, as well as Epaphras who served them for thirty years. There can be no question—Laodicea had been blessed with opportunities for growth and development, but now they were only to be pitied.

Christ appears to this church as the "Amen" who is the absolutely True One. He is the "Faithful and True Witness" in whom there is no exaggeration. He is the "Beginning of the Creation of God" who can speak with authority since He is the cause of creation itself. This letter sent to the church reveals the causes for its spiritual deterioriation. The wording in the letter indicates the fact that the church is to be pitied rather than condemned.

It was to be pitied because of its condition (Rev. 3:15). The church was neither hot nor cold. They were a perfectly harmless set of good people who were not particularly bad or good. It is hard to realize how a group of people can believe in the great truths of the ruin of man, redemption in Christ, and the responsibility of man, and be content to allow spiritual lukewarmness to characterize their endeavors for Christ and His Kingdom.

It was to be pitied because of its conversation (Rev. 3:17). The church said that it was rich and had need of nothing when actually it was miserable, poor, blind, and naked. The city had great buildings. The ruins can be seen today. The city had money. When it was destroyed in A.D. 62, it refused any outside financial assistance in rebuilding. It was known for its scientific advances including the development of the Phrygian powder and the corylium eye salve. It was well known for its productivity of glossy wool for expensive garments. Those great advances gave them a distorted view of their true condition.

It was to be pitied because of its companionships (Rev. 3:20). How sad to see their royal visitor standing outside. He had made the house of worship but could not get in. He had purchased the house but could not get through the door. Humanly speaking, Laodicea had about everything but Christ. The excluded Christ was not waiting for the vote of a board or a committee that He might gain entrance. He was waiting for one individual to open the door and He would then enter and they would have blessed fellowship together (Rev. 3:20). The church had been doing business with the world when it should have been dealing with Christ. He admonishes them to buy of Him the provision of gold refined in the fire, eye salve for the eyes, which would give them perception, and white raiment symbolic of the real purity they so desperately needed.

To those who with the help of Christ would perceive and become overcomers the promise of the greatest glory was given. They would be permitted to be seated beside the Savior on His throne. There is no greater glory. It is possible to go from riches to rags, but what a pity!

We fear that many established churches have never really analyzed their condition, conversation, and companionships to ascertain their need for revitalization. We have provided guidance in many areas of church life in the earlier chapters of this book. We recognize, however, that the church belongs to Christ and therefore He should be recognized as the foundation stone upon which it is built. The person of Christ must not be excluded from the work of His church. There can be no lasting and fully satisfying revitalization of the church without the presence and power of God.

The message to the church at Pergamum recorded in Rev. 2:12-17 tells us to employ discipline in the church in order to avoid doctrinal compromise. It is the testimony of Scripture that doctrine and duty should be combined. What we believe has an influence upon how we behave. If the activities connected with church revitalization are to be productive, then there must be no doctrinal compromise.

The Christ of the candlesticks is depicted to this church at Pergamum as the One with a two-edged sword (Rev. 2:12). He states very clearly that He has a few things against this church (Rev. 2:14) which was located on a majestic cliff in the capital of the province of Asia. The church had a dangerous minority within it needing correction and discipline.

The ones needing discipline are identified as those who held the teachings of Balaam and the teachings of the Nicolaitans. Balaam had feared God but worshiped gold as he tried to make the best of both worlds (Num. 22-25). Balaam refused the instructions of God and finally lost his life together with 24,000 Israelites (Num 31:8). The Nicolaitans preached and practiced a distortion of the doctrine of grace. They felt that the Christian was free to follow the practices of sin. Liberty meant license. That minority within the church did not keep a good line of separation between the worship of idols and the worship of the true God. They also did not keep a good line of separation in the matters of morality (Rev. 2:14-15). They had not condoned sin, but had done nothing to eradicate it.

The ones needing discipline were located within a good church. Christ knew about the environment in which they were working (Rev. 2:13) and commended the church for their loyalty. They had held fast to His name and had not denied His faith. Many good churches have had their minorities whose involvement with immorality and idolatry have brought down the displeasure of God.

Those needing discipline even within this good church had to be disciplined or the church would miss some choice blessings. The blessings would be for those who would overcome (Rev. 2:17). They would first of all receive the gift of hidden manna, which would provide extra strength for the extra mile. They would also receive a white stone. That may refer to the white stone signifying acquittal within the courts. It may refer to the *tessera hospitalis,* which was the friendship stone. It may refer to the white stone of victory. The final blessing to be received is the inscription of the new name on the stone. No one knows the expression of personality and character except the one who receives it.

The church at Pergamum had a false tolerance toward those with doctrinal error and were condemned for that tolerance. We sin when we tolerate what God condemns. When the minority sins, the majority suffers. Several have stated that the church of our day is doctrinally illiterate. If that is true, it may account for the strange behavior that has infiltrated the church of our day. One of the basics in church revitalization centers in the matter of doctrinal instruction. Doctrinal teaching and preaching have been very significant features in church revivals. Doctrinal ignorance and compromise will take the lifeblood from the church.

The message to the church at Thyatira in Revelation 2:18-29 tells us to strive for holiness in order to avoid moral compromise. The message to the church at Thyatira is the longest of the seven although Thyatira is possibly the least important church of the group. The only reference to Thyatira in the book of Acts is 16:14. The church at Thyatira at that time was strong but only in numbers. It has been said that no other city of its day had more trade guilds than Thyatira. Those were really brotherhoods based upon paganism and immorality.

That progressive church had one outstanding difficulty that kept it from claiming the full blessing of God. They had one woman in the church who called herself a prophetess and was teaching and beguiling God's servants to practice immorality and to eat food sacrificed to idols. It only takes one false teacher to disrupt the work of God. Tragedy always results from tolerating sin. Calamity always results from compromise with sin.

The tragedy of tolerating sin is evidenced in the experience of the saints. Christ knew that this was a church with many good qualities (Rev. 2:19). Their works, love, faith, service, patient endurance, and the acceleration of their present works over their previous works were all worthy of commendation. The fact is made very clear to the church that such toleration of sin would ruin their reputation and bring down the judgment of God. They were to be thrown into great tribulation if they continued to pursue peaceful coexistence with the false teacher.

The tragedy of tolerating sin is evidenced in the experience of the sinner. Jezebel called herself a prophetess. She was evidently known for her loud claims and loose living. She evidently was not trying to drive out the true worship but was rather just desirous of having an equal opportunity. "Behold, I will cast her upon a bed of sickness, and those who commit [spiritual] adultery with her into great tribulation" (Rev. 2:22).

The tragedy of tolerating sin is evidenced in the statements of the Christ of the candlesticks. He is portrayed to this church as being the One with eyes like a flame of fire and with feet of burnished bronze (Rev. 2:18). Christ makes it clear that He cannot give His blessing as long as there is toleration of sin. If, however, they hold fast to what they have and keep His works until the end, then He will give them power over the nations. Christ also promises that He will give the overcomers the Morning Star (Rev. 2:26-27). That is the promise of His personal presence. When the Morning Star appears, it brings the promise that the night is over and the day is dawning. Christ desires blessing for His people. The toleration of sin stops the blessing. There are churches where the preaching and teaching of holiness are not welcomed. The face is overlooked that we are called unto holiness and that God cannot bless ungodliness. True church revitalization must be in agreement with God's Word and must give a prominent place to the preaching, teaching, and practicing of holiness of life.

Each person is important. When one stands for the right and maintains a standard of godliness, blessings come. When one does not dare to be different and gives way to the toleration of sin in any form, then the righteous suffer, the sinner himself suffers, and worst of all the Savior cannot shower blessing upon His people. Never overlook the importance of the influence of one life for good or for evil.

The message to the church at Smyrna recorded in Rev. 2:8-11 reminds us to take courage by keeping in mind God's provisions. The book of Revelation has been classified as apocalyptic literature. One of the characteristics of such writing is that it provides encouragement to those being oppressed. That is certainly evidenced in this shortest of the seven letters. The name of the city of Smyrna means bitter, myrrh and suffering, but it was known by reputation as a city of beauty. In spite of that, Christianity held on longer there than in any other city of Asia Minor. The blood of the martyrs truly became the seed of the church. Laodicea had been a rich church but without commendation of Christ. Smyrna was a poor church but without condemnation by Christ. The Lord of the lampstands discerned the storm clouds that were gathering over the city and provided encouragement for the believers.

The first encouragement was to the effect that they had a sympathizing Savior. The Christ of the candlesticks was about to say, "fear not," as He had done so many times. Before He did, however, He clarified and affirmed the fact that He was there first (Rev. 2:8). He had been tempted in all points yet was without sin (Heb. 4:15). He was able to know that which they faced and could be sympathetic with them in their testing. He had even died and had come to life (Rev. 2:8). This sympathetic Savior knew all about their tribulation, poverty, and slander (Rev. 2:9). There are no secrets with God. The tribulation refers to the consequences that would come to them in being identified with Christ. The poverty referred to their loss of all things. The slander must have had two qualifications, namely, that it was not true and that it was endured for the sake of Christ.

The next encouragement was that they would have a limited time of trouble (Rev. 2:10). We can endure almost anything providing there is some hope that it will not continue without end. Christ here unrolls the scroll of suffering. Ten great persecutions were inflicted under the Roman Empire. The longest of those lasted ten years. No matter what the actual length was, however, Christ assured them that there was a terminal point when it would all be over.

The church was given the encouragement of a promised reward (Rev. 2:10). That crown of life was the royal crown and not the garland of victory. Just imagine their thrill as they realized that despised disciples were candidates for royal crowns. "Blessed is a man who perseveres under trial; for once he has been approved, he will receive the crown of life, which the Lord has promised to those who love Him" (James 1:12).

The final encouragement in the list was that of a promised protection (Rev. 2:11). The one who conquers will not be hurt at all by the second death. "Blessed and holy is the one who has a part in the first resurrection; over these the second death has no power" (Rev. 20:6; 20:14; 21:8). This church contributed many names to the roll of honored martyrs for Christ. One of those was Polycarp, the well-known Bishop of Smyrna. At the time of his martyrdom, he declared, "Eighty and six years have I served Jesus Christ; He has been a good master to me all these years and shall I forsake Him now?" They could separate him from his loved ones through physical death but not from his God.

This same Christ of the candlesticks provides blessings for the burdened even today. He is still a sympathizing Savior. He has assured us that soon the cares and toils of life will all be over. He has promised a reward that will not perish and a protection that is flawless. When a church undertakes the process of revitalization, trials may come. There may be some who really do not want the church to get down to business because they do not want to invest their time, talent, and treasure. Any worthwhile activity takes sacrifice. That word will disturb many. When disturbances and problems arise during the process of revitalization, it is helpful to remember the encouragements given to the church at Smyrna during its days of trial.

The message to the church at Philadelphia in Revelation 3:7-13 says that the church should take advantage of its God-given opportunities. Philadelphia was the keeper of the gateway to the Phrygian land and Great Central Plateau. It was quite appropriate in view of the geographical location as well as for other reasons that the postman of Patmos should deliver an epistle to the church at Philadelphia with the pleasant news that there had been set before the church an open door that no one could shut (Rev. 3:8).

This terminology of the open door occurs quite often in Scripture. An open door was opened for Paul in Corinth (1 Cor. 16:9; 2 Cor. 2:12-13). Paul prayed that an open door might be found at Colossae (Col. 4:3). The door that had been opened at Philadelphia had been opened by the Lord. Those are doors through which we may well pass and for which we should be forever grateful. Doors opened by Satan should be avoided at all costs. The church at Philadelphia was commended for having dealt wisely with its open door.

The author of the letter commends the church for using the power they possessed. He knew that they did not have too much, but they had used what they had (3:8b). They had also kept Christ's Word and had not denied His name. Since they had used the potential at their disposal, the promise was given that those of the synagogue of Satan who had opposed them would be brought to worship at their feet (3:9). They were also promised that they would be kept from the hour of tribulation. Christ does not condemn His people for scarcity but does commend them for making profitable use of that which they have.

The church at Philadelphia was also encouraged to use the promises available for fulfillment. The first of those promises assures them that if they were to overcome, they would be made pillars in the House of the Lord. The pillar is a very vital part of any building and the weight of the building rests upon it. They were to be given a position of permanence within the temple of God. The stamp of God's ownership and likeness was also to be placed upon them (Rev. 3:12b). Their citizenship was to be clearly established and defined. The name of the city of God, the New Jerusalem that will come down out of Heaven from God, was to be written upon them. The final promise was that God would reveal the new name. He has a name that no one knows but Himself (Rev. 19:12). Just the remembrance of those four great promises made to the overcomer should serve as motivation for heightened service. He promises a permanent position in His temple, ownership, citizenship, and a glorious revelation. He always keeps His promises.

This church at Philadelphia had kept its commitments to God, now God assures them that He is going to keep His commitment to them. The One who was revealed to this church as having the key to the House of David where the treasures of the King were kept (Rev. 3:7) could assure this church that when He opened the door, none could shut it (Isa. 22:22). Hold fast that which you have that no one take your crown of reward (Rev. 3:11). This is a day of opportunity for the church. The needs are great, and the promises of God are sure.

There has never been a significant time of social, political, or religious renewal without oratory. Oratory that is able to stir hope of a better condition and point the way to achieving that hope is a vital element of parish revitalization. Preaching possesses the potential to kill or to bring to life. Preaching that demonstrates a clear connection between the elements of a revitalization process, the Word of God, and corporate worship brings new life to the congregation by unifying all of the resources of the church in pursuit of the ministries and goals the congregation has set for itself.

You can do much to strengthen the results of assessment, goal-setting, and budgeting by *preaching* about assessment, goal-setting and budgeting. In this chapter we have attempted to show you how that type of preaching is done. Some of our students and colleagues are connecting their preaching to parish revitalization processes with good results. One of the best examples we have seen of this was given to us by Dr. Clifford Anderson, executive for home missions, General Conference Baptist Church. Cliff led a congregation through the assessment process described in chapter 1. Before beginning the assessment on a Sunday afternoon he preached a sermon on assessment. A detailed outline of that sermon is given below. Similar preaching can be done to enable the congregation to see that the Word is being expressed in all of the parish revitalization processes.

Subject: Analysis   Preaching Portion: Revelation 2:1-7
Theme: How to Do an Analysis
Intro.: "If you don't care where you are going, any road will get you there." It is always appropriate to analyze or evaluate the present status of an organization so that there can be progress with purpose.

Explanation:
1. Rev. 2:1-7 is the demonstrable concern of Christ for a first century church in the province of Asia.
2. As a church, others had appropriately shared with them a sense of direction, c.f., St. Paul, c.f., Acts 18, 19; Ephesians.
3. Reputed to have influenced the entire province of Asia for good.
4. In Rev. 2:1-7, Christ the head of the church leads the church of Ephesus to see their strengths, their weaknesses and the hope or dream for this first century church.
5. The relevancy and application of this process to the twentieth century church is seen in Rev. 2:7a.

Prop.: It is important that we understand the process of self-assessment.
T.S.: You and I can understand the process of self-assessment by giving attention to the steps of that process as modeled by the risen Christ.
I. *First step in the process is the identification of the church's strengths* (Rev. 2:2, 3)

Proclamational Aspects of Revitalization • 135

1. The works or activity of the church that bore positive results are noted as a strength.
2. The investment of time and energies on the part of the members are noted as a strength.
3. Their patience in a difficult environment is an identifiable strength.
4. Corporate purity—uprooting evil within the church and standing against evil outside the church—is a strength.
5. Persevering in righteousness—courageous strength and endurance in the context of evil. They were salt, light, life in a decadent society—a strength.
6. They opposed the deeds of the Nicolaitans who advocated their liberty as license to sin.

II. Second step in the process is the church's weaknesses—Rev. 2:4
1. Activity trap had replaced *agape* love.
2. Early demonstrations of love for God and their brothers had been replaced by a search for heresy. Suspicion had dulled their first love.
3. The Body of Christ had ceased to be the complete expression of the Savior's love.

III. Third step in the process is the expression of Christ's hope for the church—Rev. 2:5—Three words that express that hope:
1. Remember—what an aid memory is in correction.
2. Repent—a reversal of present course is called for.
3. Repeat—do the first works.

Rev. 2:1-7 is a statement of direction. It is not difficult to identify the strengths, weaknesses, hopes, and dreams for the church as Christ models the process. Therefore, we might well give ourselves to determining what Christ's direction for our church might be by pursuing the process of identifying our strengths, our weaknesses, and our hopes and dreams. May God give us the grace to see our church as He sees us.

NOTES

1. Findley B. Edge, *The Greening of the Church* (Waco, Tex.: Word, 1971), pp. 13-14.
2. Lyle Schaller, *The Local Church Looks to the Future* (Nashville: Abingdon, 1968), pp. 21-64.
3. Lloyd M. Perry, *Biblical Preaching for Today's World* (Chicago: Moody, 1973). See also Charles W. Koller, *Expository Preaching Without Notes, Plus Sermons Preached Without Notes* (Grand Rapids: Baker, 1962).
4. A. W. Tozer, *The Presence of God* (Harrisburg, Pa.: Christian Publications, 1948), p. 128.
5. G. Campbell Morgan, *The Corinthian Letters of Paul* (Westwood, N. J.: Revell, 1946), pp. 144-61.
6. Hans-Ruedi Weber, "The Training of the Laity for Their Ministry in the World," *The Laity,* June 1956, p. 5.
7. Alfred Lord Tennyson, *The Poems and Plays of Alfred Lord Tennyson* (New York: Random, Modern Library, 1938), p. 65.
8. G. Campbell Morgan, *The Letters of Our Lord: A First Century Message to the Twentieth Century Christians* (London: Pickering & Inglis, 1964).

9

Theological Reflection on Church Revitalization Process

> To do theology is to try to see things as God sees them. The task is so obviously arrogant and oversized that we can only do it playfully, as children. But to children play is serious and creative, and it does something to the growth.[1]

To theologize about revitalization is to think seriously about the needs of the world around us, our church, our own leadership styles, and whether we lead the church in such a way that it is engaging those needs or ignoring them. To do theology is to try to see all of this, and more, as God might see it.[2]

The first question one might ask is, "Does God actually think about planning cycles, organizational structures, and leadership at all?" The answer is an absolute yes. Scripture is filled with material telling us He is concerned that the plans and organization of His church be effective and that they model His basic requirements of all human structures: love, truth, and justice. The Ten Commandments are commandments to observe love, truth, and justice. They apply to organizations as well as to individuals.

Have you ever thought of the fact that organizational structures, themselves, can be loving or unloving, truthful or untruthful, just or unjust? Those characteristics are not reserved for individuals alone. They are also present in the organization structures and policies people set up to carry out their work.

Scripture gives some striking illustrations of God's interest in the plans and organizational structures His people put together to carry out their ministry. For example, Exodus 18:13-27 gives us an illustration of an ineffective structure Moses had established to govern the congregation of Israel. God graciously sent Jethro to Moses with suggestions for a completely new structure.

God also demonstrated a great deal of interest in the organizations of the New Testament church, such as the installation of the first deacon board in Acts 6. As the church grew in numbers of people and in its ministries, Paul spent a good deal of time establishing organizational policies and structures to keep the church effective. In those teachings we find God has both a healthy interest and involvement in setting up the offices and policies of the early church, for example, Eph. 4:11, 12 lists the offices He instituted and 2 Timothy 5:17-25, Titus 1:15-16, describe some of the policies those persons and the church were to follow.

A study of Scripture regarding organizational structure and policy quickly convinces us God is indeed interested in the way we organize the church. Some of the measuring sticks by which He judges church organizations are: is the organization effective, and are its structures and policies fully loving, truthful, and just?

Reflecting on the Revitalization Process

If God is interested in the structures we put together to carry out our ministry, we should be too. At a minimum we should measure them against scriptural standards for love, truth, and justice.

1. Are the revitalization processes suggested in this book loving? Providing the laity with effective church structures through which they can discover their own calling in ministry and then effectively carry out their ministry is one of the most loving things any pastor and church may do for the congregation.

Unfortunately, many pastors have been taught to believe that they can only express love to persons through personal contact. Consequently, they put their attention to counseling or visitation. Those are most assuredly of great importance and not to be neglected, but one can also express love by providing the congregation with structures that work!

The revitalization processes discussed in this book are loving in nature. When persons are given the opportunity to participate in clarifying the mission of their church, in creating the plans to achieve that mission, and in finding their place in carrying out those plans, and when all the resources of the church are aligned to ensure their success in that place of ministry, they are being loved and they know it.

It makes good sense for a busy pastor to love the people through organizational structures. In a counseling session the pastor is typically involved with only one or two people at a time. However, the pastor can express the same degree of love and acceptance for one hundred or one thousand people at one time by providing them an opportunity to participate in a congregational assessment where the entire congregation can work together to chart the future of their church.

2. *Are the organizations of our church fully truthful? Are all our actions fully consistent with our theology and preaching?* In his profound book, *Truthfulness, the Future of the Church,* Hans Küng says

> In one way or another truthfulness is a problem which concerns every church . . . By truthfulness we mean much more than sincerity or honesty in the narrow sense. We mean, first of all, that basic attitude through which individuals or communities (organizations), in spite of difficulties, remain true to themselves without dissimulation and without losing their integrity: a genuine candor with oneself, with one's fellows and with God, genuine candor in thought, word and deed.[3]

In that same book Mr. Küng says, "With the Second Vatican Council came the 'moment of truth' for the Catholic Church. . . ." He is referring to the fact that the council came to be one in which the church leaders had to openly confront the viability of the church structures for a modern world and the subservient role to which laity were being relegated. Facing the moment of truth is not easy for any church. "One day during a session of the Second Vatican Council, one bishop passed another a note, which then made the rounds. The message read, 'The Senate does not make mistakes, and if it does, it does not correct them, lest it should seem to have erred.' "[4]

Küng is right. The Catholic church is not alone in the difficulty of making its organizational structures and policies fully truthful, and the moment of truth has arrived for Protestant denominations as well as the Catholic church. Many of our practices and policies are not fully consistent with our preaching, for example pastors who preach "love for the brethren" but complain about their congregations to one another. We have personally observed many situations in evangelical churches in which organizations were not truthful. When a church board keeps secrets from the congregation it is not being truthful. When the finance committee presents financial reports that hide information or confuse the people, it is not being truthful. Watergate was a vivid portrayal of a leader who organized to willfully deceive the people. We have seen dozens of "Watergates" in churches with which we have worked.

The revitalization processes suggested in this book are designed to enable the church to be fully truthful. Using these methods, all the members are allowed to speak their views without intimidation, plans are created free from manipulation, and weaknesses in existing programs are identified and corrected in a spirit of honest inquiry and search for a better way to perform the church's ministry.

3. *Do the organizations of our church model justice for all persons in our congregation, community, and world?* There is little justice in expecting members of the church to support programs they have had no opportunity to help create. There is little justice in organizing the church in such a way that the majority of the laity must be silent and passive.

During a worship service, generally only the pastor is active. The laity are expected to come, but to passively, silently watch the pastor in action. It is in the church organizations that the laity can be most active. The church has perfected lay ministry opportunities in the Sunday school. Here many lay persons have become active. Unfortunately, the church has done quite poorly beyond the Sunday school, the women's group, and administrative board.

The revitalization processes discussed in this book, however, provide structures in which all members can be fully active in planning, supporting, and working to carry out the church's ministry. This is justice in action, for no person is asked to support either with time or money any programs he has not helped to create.

The Important Place of Clergy and Laity in Church Organizations

The Old Testament presents three major kinds of ministry: prophet, priest, and king. Each of those ministries, although very different, were nonetheless ministries to people. The priest ministered to the private and spiritual needs. The prophet ministered to the public, social, and religious needs. The king ministered to organizational and political needs. The king's ministry was to manage wisely and effectively the human organizational resources put under his care by God.

There was, of course, some overlap in the way the ministers carried out their ministries. David, for example, wrote many priestly psalms, although he was a king not a priest. God held each of the three ministries to be of equal importance and intended them to be supportive of one another.

Only one of the Old Testament ministries required ordination, the priestly ministry. The other two were ministries of the laity. All, however, clergy and laity alike, were called by God and were of equal status in the eyes of God.

In the New Testament God laid upon Christ all three of these ministries; He became prophet, priest, and king. Not only did Christ accept those three ministries as one, but He provided for the continuation of this three-in-one ministry by calling pastors and laying upon them the charge to minister in His stead to whatever local church they were called. The management/leadership functions of the pastor's role are as much a part of the call, and as important to the growth of the church, as the priestly and prophetic functions Christ lays upon them. A pastor who shuns this work is shunning the full call Christ has given, and crippling the church as much as if he did not tend to preaching or praying. God apparently thinks highly of a ministry to and through the organizational structures of the church. But the pastor does not have to be involved in leading every program in the church. Moses presents a shining example of the ills that come when the leader structures the organization so he can be involved in every decision and program. A careful reading of Exodus 18:13-27 shows the foolishness and danger of the pastor's "trying to run the whole show." We will paraphrase the Scripture.

The next day Moses took his seat to run the show. When Jethro saw this he said, "What are you doing? This is not the way to lead these people. You will only wear yourself out and the people will be worse off too. Now, listen, there is a better way. It is for you to be the people's representative before God—your chief business is to pray for them, and preach to them God's Word and teach them how to live and act. Beyond that you must structure the organization so that the people, themselves, become the ministers. You are not the only one who can help these people, Moses. Wise up! If you do this God will give you strength, and all these people will be revitalized together with you."

Jesus also demonstrated these organizational principles. He structured His fledgling group so that every single person had a significant ministry, and He set them free to do it on their own. He always gave them His support, but never His interference. When they made mistakes or failed He did not take their ministry away. Rather, He used their failures as opportunities to prepare them for an even more effective ministry. Luke gives two such accounts; the sending of the twelve in chapter 9, and the sending of the seventy in chapter 10. For an example of His using failure to prepare for even greater ministry, see Mark 9:14-29.

The pastor should not have to be involved in every program or every decision. When the pastor insists upon being involved in everything the church will always be weaker and smaller than it would be otherwise, for the church will be limited to the extent of the pastor's abilities and available time. The church will never grow beyond his strengths and abilities. The tragedy is that the talents of many of the laity will be wasted from inactivity and nonuse.

Pastors who teach the people to follow Christ's example should do likewise, not only in his priestly and prophetic role, but also regarding his ministry as manager and leader. Pastor, set your people free to do their own ministry! Call them, inspire them, and equip them, and set them free to do their ministry on their own—with your full support but not your interference. And while they are ministering, you are called to pray unceasingly for them and the success of their ministry. That is your chief responsibility. You will find the time to pray when you are no longer trying to attend every meeting, make every decision, and run every program.

First Corinthians 12 declares all are members of the Body of Christ, each with his own function. All are ministers, from the least conspicuous member to the noted leaders of the church (vs. 12-23). To each one God has given a gift for service, vs. 4-7; and a special ministry, vs. 28-31. The pastor is not the only minister, but is one minister among many and to whom has been given the responsibility of enabling all others to discover and use their own unique gifts and calling in effective ministry.

Each local church is uniquely chosen by God to be His body in that place. His is an active body, with every member assigned a specific ministry to perform. In order to carry on those many ministries the church must organize itself for action in such a way that every member becomes active in ministry. It must pray for the Spirit of God to fill every minister and anoint every ministry—then the church of the twentieth century will be revitalized, and not until them.

Organizing the Church to Set Persons Free

A major result of our Lord's ministry was to set people free from whatever fear, passion, or institution enslaved them. So central was that to His purpose in coming that He began His ministry with this declaration: "THE SPIRIT OF THE LORD IS UPON ME, BECAUSE . . . HE HAS SENT ME TO PROCLAIM RELEASE TO THE CAPTIVES . . ." (Luke 4:18). Again in John 8:36 He asserts this purpose in His ministry, "If therefore the Son shall make you free, you shall be free indeed."

Paul took up the touchy subject of freedom in a slave-holding society and what it meant in the relationship of a slave and master when once they both had been set free by Christ (see Paul's letter to Philemon).

It is the purpose of Christ to set persons free from sin, sickness, boredom, enslaving institutions (even if they be religious institutions), and all things that might restrict the freedom He purchased for the sons and daughters of God.

It is unfortunate that many pastors work to set people free from spiritual bondage, then work to keep them in servitude to denominational policies and their own wishes regarding the church programs. Think for a moment of the many complaints you have heard from pastors regarding members who are not supporting their pet programs, who do not accept responsibilities as they are asked, who stay away from meetings.

On the other hand, congregations often attempt to control and enslave the pastor. They complain about his preaching, leadership, the terrible behavior of the children, and of the condition of the parsonage. Persons who complain and find fault with the pastor should ponder the dim attitude God took toward Miriam and Aaron for their complaining about Moses, Numbers 12:1-10, and the account of Korah and his friends who complained about Moses' leadership, Numbers 16:1-38. Verse 38 makes it clear that God regards such behavior as sin, for which Korah and company paid with their lives.

In *Life Together*, Bonhoeffer asserts that it is a sin for a pastor to complain, either to other pastors or to God, about the congregation God put in his care. He urges pastors to be careful lest they should even complain to God in their prayers.[5] When the pastor complains about the congregation it is generally because the people are resisting some decision or action he is trying to enforce upon them against their will. Such attempts to control people are enslaving in nature. The same care needs to be exercised by laity in relationship to their pastor.

The revitalization processes discussed in this book set pastor and people free from any attempt to dominate, to enforce their will over the other. In this process all persons are equally free to participate in planning and carrying out the church's ministry.

Chris Argyris, Professor at Harvard University, has developed a three-phase plan for instituting creative change in a modern organization.[6] He lists the steps as follows:

1. Generate valid and useful information about the organization or situation you want to change.
2. Allow the members of the organization to make free and informed choices (plans) regarding the changes to be made, based upon the information generated in step one.
3. Motivate personal commitment on the part of the people to the choices they have made.

Argyris says these are progressive steps. The members cannot make informed decisions if they do not have valid and useful information; and in an organization where valid and useful information is provided to enable the members to make free and informed choices, those members will develop a deepening commitment to support the decisions and programs of the organization.

This is a three-step approach to revitalizing an organization. and is a foundational theory to every process suggested in this book. For example, the mission clarification and congregational assessment are designed to generate valid and useful information about the church and community. Goal setting and implementation carried on by lay committees and task forces allows the members to make free and informed choices about the church and its ministries. A result of this is that the people are personally committed to the decisions and programs since they had a vital part in generating the information and planning the programs.

The three-step approach is also used in the suggestions regarding the recruitment and assigning of lay workers. The position description is intended to give information about the purpose and responsibilities of the job. The principle of visiting personally with the person before he is appointed to the job allows free and informed choice. The signing of the ministry covenant and the commissioning ceremony are designed to motivate internal commitment to the job once the worker accepts it.

The process set forth in this book are in keeping with Christ's ministry to set persons free. These are processes free of manipulation. Persons are free to participate or to withdraw, they are free to find their own level of involvement and their own place of ministry, all within the context of the Christian community. These processes stress collaboration and joint effort. They do not spawn "Long Rangers" or prima donnas, either among the clergy or laity.

We think God might look upon such processes as right and good for the church. What do you think?

A "View of Persons" in the Church

McGregor has suggested a leader within an organization can hold one of two views regarding the members of the organization. He has termed those views "Theory X" and "Theory Y."[7]

A "Theory X" pastor or church leader tends to view the members as being basically:
1. Unable to formulate creative, good plans for the future of the church.
2. Unable to formulate creative solutions for church problems.
3. In need of constant supervision on whatever job they have in the church.
4. Lazy and desire to do as little as necessary to keep the church operating.
5. Unable to discern the will of God for the church in any particular situation, and to respond appropriately.

A leader holding this view of the members of the church will tend to:
1. Structure and administer the church as a "directive" organization in which directions are set at the top and trickle down to the committees and members.
2. Control the decisions made regarding church programs and problems.
3. Restrict persons' freedom to act independently on their jobs.
4. Unilaterally discern and announce the will of God for the church.
5. Appoint and direct persons into positions he has decided is best for them and the church.

A Theory X leader would not subscribe to the Argyris three-step model for creative change in an organization. Rather the Theory X leader would feel a necessity to limit and control whatever information is shared with the members, control all decision-making processes, and use external and extrinsic, not internal and intrinsic, means of securing members' commitment to the church programs.

A "Theory Y" leader, on the other hand, tends to view the members as being basically:
1. Willing and able to formulate creative plans for the future of the church.
2. Capable of formulating creative solutions for the problems of the church.

3. Capable to do a good job on their own without constant direction and supervision.
4. Interested in the welfare of the church and willing to freely give of themselves to make the church effective in all of its ministries.
5. Open to the leading of the Spirit regarding the will of God, and able to respond to that leading.

A leader holding this view of the members of the church will tend to:

1. Structure and administer the church as a developmental organization in which directions are set collaboratively by the leaders and members.
2. Allow decisions to be made at every level of the church by those who have the best information and knowledge about that particular program or problem.
3. Give each person an area in which to act independently in search for creative and satisfactory ways to carry out his responsibilities.
4. Trust the member's discernment of the will of God for the church.
5. Provide structures in which members can personally decide God's call to themselves regarding the ministry He is appointing them to do.

A Theory Y leader operates in harmony with the Argyris three-step model for creative change in an organization since he trusts the members to always work for the church's best interests, has confidence in their ability to make wise decisions, and naturally assumes they will be personally committed to those decisions so long as they are provided valid and useful information and given the freedom to make informed choices.

What do you think? Is God Theory X or Theory Y in His relationships with persons and institutions? Is it the nature of God to expect the best, or the worst of persons? Does He lead in such a way as to give people freedom and responsibility, or to restrict them?

There is a story we used to hear in sermons about a conversation Christ had with an angel shortly after His resurrection and ascension:

Angel: You paid a great price to offer salvation to all people, and Your idea to carry it on through the work of the church was a good plan, but what provisions did You make for it to continue after Your ascension?

Christ: Well, I chose twelve persons, fishermen and tax collectors mostly, and I spent about three years training them to carry on in My place. Actually, there are only eleven since one betrayed Me.

Angel: Do You mean You left Your great plan and ministry in the hands of eleven uneducated and untrustworthy men! What will You do if they fail? Surely You must have another plan.

Christ: No, I have no other plan.

If Christ could entrust His entire plan to the care of the eleven surely you can trust the members of your congregation with the plans and programs of your church. Geothe once said, "Treat people as if they are what they ought to be, and you help them become what they are capable of becoming." We think the processes discussed in this book came close to doing that. We believe God might just think that's what the church ought to be doing.

Notes

1. Krister Standahl, Dean, Harvard Divinity School, in a lecture in Shalom Center, Sioux Falls, South Dakota, 1979.
2. While writing this book we became familiar with another little book that is given entirely to a sensitive theological reflection on church planning and organizational structures. We highly commend Charles R. Wilson, *Sojourners in the Land of Promise: Theology, Planning and Surprise* (Downers Grove, Ill.: Organization Resources, 1981).
3. Hans Küng, *Truthfulness, the Future of the Church* (New York: Sheed & Ward, 1968), pp. 18, 20-21. Küng is a Catholic priest and seminary professor who has strongly questioned the will of the organized Christian church to be truthful. He was censored by his own church in 1980 for refusing to soften his criticism of the church.
4. Ibid., pp. 10, 15.

5. Dietrich Bonhoeffer, *Life Together* (New York: Harper & Row, 1954), pp. 29-30.
6. Chris Argyris, *Management and Organization Development* (New York: McGraw-Hill, 1971).
7. Douglas McGregor, *The Human Side of Enterprise* (New York: McGraw-Hill, 1960).

Conclusion

We said in the introduction to this book that this would be a beginning word regarding revitalization, but not the last word on the subject. Perhaps it would be more correct to say this has been an intermediate work, not first or the last.

We, with you, believe the first step toward a new life in Christ is to accept Him as Lord and Savior, that is to decide in His favor, to accept His love and forgiveness, and to orient one's entire life in His direction. That is only the beginning, however. Persons and congregations must go beyond this, for as Paul so capably argued, God's newborn children are not to spend their lives trying to be born over and over again, but are to go on from repentance to maturity and fruitfulness (see Heb. 6:1-2; 10:24; Titus 3:14).

The first step in the Christian way is to receive new life, eternal life. The second step is to keep that experience ever vital in one's life by maturing in the faith and finding one's place in the mission and ministry of God to the world. Paul knew that and therefore instructed Titus, "And let our people also learn to engage in good deeds to meet pressing needs, that they may not be unfruitful" (Titus 3:14). As persons and congregations come to do this they discover new meaning and vitality in their Christian experience. They are vitalized and revitalized again and again.

We have attempted to make it a fundamental premise of this book that before the congregation will be willing and able to invest all of its resources in doing "good deeds to meet pressing needs" the people must catch a vision that they can indeed represent Christ in the face of those needs. We have also said God chooses to give visions of and directions for ministry only to those who are already making plans and setting about to do ministry. Many congregations never experience vitality beyond the initial conversion experience because they never take a good hard look at the many pressing needs all around them that cry out for Christ's response. "But," they would say, "God is not leading us to do anything about them." "But what if we do the wrong thing? How can we be sure God wants us to get involved in the affairs of our community and world?" Remember God gave Paul his marvelous call and vision while he was busily engaged in what he thought was an important and valid ministry. He was wrong, but God did not cast him away for that. Rather, He used what Paul was already doing as the means to redirect his ways (see Acts 9).

Do you think it strange that the Lord would choose Paul, misguided and mean as he was, rather than someone else who had a bit better outlook? Apparently God finds it easier to work with someone (or a congregation) that is already doing something than with one whose attitude is, "Lord, I'll do something, anything, as soon as you show me what I should do."

Another example in Paul's life may serve to illustrate the point that God directs only those who are already actively engaged in ministry. In Acts 16 we are told a bit about his second missionary journey. "And when they had come to Mysia, they were trying [making all plans and efforts] to go into Bithynia, and the spirit of Jesus did not permit them . . . and a vision appeared to Paul in the night: a certain man of Macedonia was standing and appealing to him, and saying, 'Come over to Macedonia and help us' " (Acts 16:7, 9).

Do you begin to understand? God can only lead you when you are on the way. He will only give you a vision of the pressing needs and of ministry when you are already studying the needs and doing ministry. He cannot lead those who are not traveling. He cannot direct those who are doing nothing.

Because we believe this, we have urged you and your congregation to move beyond repentance to "engage in good deeds to meet pressing needs." It is only in that that your church can be revitalized. That is the crucial step beyond repentance. This is not to take anything away from prayer, worship, or baptism. Certainly those are the foundational essentials. They alone, however, are not sufficient to keep a church vital and responsive to the leading of God.

In this book we have suggested the planning process with substantial follow-through on the plans as a means by which God may find it possible to give your congregation a vision of the ministries He is calling it to do and to direct it in the actual doing of the ministries. This entire process of doing good deeds to meet pressing needs—to receiving a new vision of opportunities—to being led by God to capture the opportunities is what might be called the intermediate step in revitalization. As thrilling as all of this might be, God has something more for His church.

In Numbers 16:6-8, God says:

> If there is a prophet among you,
> I, the Lord, shall make Myself
>   known to him in a vision.
> I shall speak with him in a dream.
>
> Not so, with My servant Moses,
> He is faithful in all My household;
>
> With him I speak mouth to mouth,
> Even openly, and not in dark sayings,
> And he beholds the form of the
>   Lord.

That is the way it is with God. He leads us from life to life. Repentance and all the elementary aspects of the Christian life, as grand and essential as they are, are merely the beginning of our life with Him and are intended to give way to dreams and visions, which in turn give way to good deeds and all that is essential to a mature Christian life (see James 2:14-18).

But even that is not all there is to God's plan. For beyond all visions and dreams we may bring into reality—God has yet a final step in His plan of revitalization. To Moses and to every faithful one is the promise that the day is coming when He will speak to us face to face (no need for visions then) as we at last behold in clear view the person of our Lord.

Appendix A

OUTLINE FOR HOME MEETING NO. 1

PREPARATION

Materials: Name tags, pens, information cards, larger paper and markers.

Purpose: To gather the persons who have been assigned to you to discuss:
1. "What are the strengths of our church?" (What do we have going for us?)
2. "What are the weaknesses of our church?" (What do we have going against us?)
3. "What are our hopes and dreams for our church?"

ACTUAL MEETING

(Meet and greet each person as they arrive. Ask each person to wear a name tag. As people are assembling, you can ask them to fill out the Information Card, which is an attempt to update our mailing list—one card per family.)

Production Minutes: (When all have gathered, briefly explain why we are gathered.) As you know from the pulpit announcements and from the letters sent to all the parishioners we have come together this evening to share our feelings and thoughts about our congregation.

Goal:	All the parishioners are being asked to contribute their ideas and feelings about our church so that all of us together can make our church the kind of parish that will help each of us to deepen, to express, and to share our faith in Christ with each other.
Background:	We have been able to gather tonight because some of our fellow members have been working to plan just how the whole church family could most effectively be reached so that each attender could contribute his feelings and ideas about our church.
Contacts:	A couple of weeks ago we volunteered to act as contact persons. We were given a list of people in this area to contact and to invite to a meeting such as this. The purpose of our meeting is to explore together how each of us sees our church and to ask ourselves what each of us would like to see our church become.
Approach:	The way we would like to go about this task is two-fold. First, we would like to discuss the three questions in the order given. Second, a recorder will list all items shared under each of the three categories.
	The results will be made available to all our church attenders. We hope that small group discussions such as ours tonight will provide a good picture of what we all want our church to be. Once we have this picture, we can all begin working to make our church the kind of Christian community that will assist each of us to deepen, to express, and to share his belief in Christ.
Discussion:	Each of us is here tonight because each of us in our own way values our participation in Bethel. It is important for us to share our views about Bethel with each other so that, together we can construct the kind of church community which will be of service to all of us.

	In a moment we will divide ouselves into two groups of about six or seven persons.
Question #1: (30 min.)	What we would like to do now is to ask you to focus on this question:

> What are the strengths of our church?
> (What do we have going for us?)

We ask one person in each group to play "participant-recorder" by taking down the ideas and feelings expressed. If you're recording, don't forget to voice your own views, too!

Question #2: We now focus our attention on the question:
(30 min.)

> What are the weaknesses of our church?
> (What do we have going against us?)

Participant-recorder continues in that role.

Question #3: We focus on:
(30 min.)

> What are our hopes and dreams for Bethel?

Participant-recorder continues in that role.

Refreshments: The group leader will call us back together to share our findings. (If possible, coffee might be served at this time.)

Conclusion: We have all spent some time this evening discussing our mutual hopes and concerns for Bethel. What we would like to do now is have each group take about five minutes to briefly share their findings.

Hear: Reports

Ask: "What are the similarities and differences?"

As we mentioned earlier, the survey results will be tabulated in the next couple weeks and will be made available to the entire congregation.

Appendix B

A sample of one category, with its listing of strengths, weaknesses, hopes and dreams, and the descriptive statements prepared for that category.

NOTE: The numerals behind a statement indicate the number of small groups that listed that particular statement.

VI. *FELLOWSHIP*

Strengths
1. Caring is expressed with each other (9)
2. Friendly (5)
3. Good fellowship—love, community, feeling of being wanted and needed leads to response of giving (3)
4. A lot of acceptance and love among people (3)
5. Deacon's fund—meeting people's physical needs (2)
6. Prayer chain is good
7. Joy in fellowship
8. Women's Circle provides strength in fellowship
9. Fellowship dinners and picnics—opportunity to know people better
10. Show great concern for familes and their needs
11. Congregation makes an effort to know new-comers
12. Fellowship potlucks
13. Companionship of the church

Weaknesses
1. Lack of social activities (fun nights)—young marrieds,

all age groups, single adults (20-27), men's fellowship (6)
2. Need more inter-member fellowship (5)
3. Lack of friendliness to newcomers (4)
4. Hurt feelings (differences in thoughts and beliefs) and lack of willingness to work things out (3)
5. Some say the church is not friendly
6. We aren't "people helpers"—shut-ins, divorcees, sick people
7. Care of the stricken. Who meets their needs?
8. Lack of reaching out and being responsive to others
9. Lack of specific system of getting to know others
10. Meeting needs of single adults socially

Hopes and Dreams

1. Interdependence within the body—sense of community (4)
2. Development of a parish-shepherd program (3)
3. More caring and sharing for other people's burdens and needs (3)
4. More regular social activities for single adults (2)
5. Fun fellowships: sports, picnics, bike progressive dinners, boating, swimming, skiing, rollerskating (2)
6. More visitation of members (2)
7. Greater sense of community (2)
8. A time of fellowship on Sunday mornings (2)
9. Church sports
10. Closer fellowship extended to newcomers
11. More potlucks in homes and church
12. Hotline—communicating needs so that the church can meet them
13. More warmth between people after services
14. Have farewell fellowships for members moving away and no exemptions
15. Improved visitation program ("shepherds" system)
16. Means of mobilizing people for service to others (for example, if sick, mow lawn)
17. Father-son socials (list of boys interested)
18. Encourage fellowship in the foyer
19. Men's fellowship

20. More social events on weekends (alternatives to secular movies, etc.)
21. A time for the church just to be open to have sharing times with others.

Descriptive Statement on Fellowship

Although there are many who feel that there is strength in caring, love, and acceptance of each other in this church, there are others who feel that this is a definite weakness. This is expressed in two areas: social interaction and burden bearing.

People are asking for a friendlier atmosphere after the church services on Sunday, social contacts to include potlucks in homes and church, fun fellowships such as sports, picnics, bike progressive dinners, and father-son socials. We need a means of mobilizing people such as a hotline to communicate people's needs for burden-bearing.

Appendix C

ACCOUNTING PRACTICES

CASH FLOW CHART

It is essential that the church establish a cash flow chart. That covers anticipated income and expenditures. That will enable the church to pay its bills each month as they are received. Each church has an individual pattern of income and expenses that can be rather accurately anticipated. The flow of funds into a church treasury is seasonal. There is a huge increase at Christmas and Easter and a rather drastic drop in the summer. Expenses do go on all year, even in the summer, but offerings just do not come in evenly.

Estimate the income for each month and decrease it by 1 percent as a safety factor. You can then assume that the church should not plan to spend more money in a given month than the total anticipated income for that month. That way you can determine which expenses should be postponed until a later month in the year.

A specific person should be charged with the responsibility of buying all goods and services needed by the church. Only that individual should have the authority to obligate the congregation for payment. In a small congregation one of the members of the board of trustees may act as purchasing agent.

When the congregation appoints someone to act as purchasing agent, it must clearly define his responsibility and authority. In actual practice the purchasing agent may delegate authority to others for purchasing certain items. It is reasonable, for example, to have the custodian be responsible for determining kinds and quality of cleaning materials to be purchased and even to place routine orders for such items with vendors approved by the purchasing agent. A purchasing agent should keep a current list of suppliers from whom goods and services needed by the church can be purchased. That list shows the names of vendors who are suitable to supply the needs of the church. Over a period of years such a list will show reputable firms with whom church purchasing agents can deal with confidence.

Financial aspects are important to the process of revitalization. Their importance can be emphasized by having the church celebrate each major financial step taken and each financial victory gained. The people waited upon God for His direction. He provided the means for achieving the goals and carrying out the planning process. A spiritual celebration should mark each financial victory.

The purchasing process begins with a requisition. The requisition is the form used by the individuals within the organization to communicate their needs to the purchasing agent. Before the requisition is actually used by the purchasing agent, it must be scrutinized by the department chairman who is responsible for that portion of the church budget. If the chairman is convinced that the need is legitimate and if he knows that he has enough money in the budget to cover the cost, he will approve the requisition and forward it to the purchasing agent.

PURCHASING

Purchasing should be a centralized function. Those who use the materials should have a decision in selecting them. Supplies and equipment must be so handled that there are checks and balances at each step from their selection to the time they are used or become obsolete. Purchasing should be so organized that the user will have the right quantity of what he needs and at the right time. There should be sufficient flexibility in the purchasing program to allow for experimentation or for a change in program or for emergencies. Members have a right to expect the greatest possible return from every church dollar spent. Records of the purchasing office should be open to the members for scrutiny. No activities should take place that throw a cloud of suspicion on the integrity of the congregation. The purchasing system should be used to spend church funds in accordance with the adopted budget.

A church in financial difficulty must increase income and control expenditures. When those steps are not taken, deficit spending results, and that can continue for only a limited time. Churches have found it profitable to employ some of the following suggestions in their attempt to keep expenditures within a reasonable boundary.

Control System. It is imperative that an authorization control system be employed in connection with the church budget. It is preferable to have a controller for each segment of the budget rather than one for the entire budget. Designate that controller by office rather than by name. You now have one person who is responsible if a particular portion of your budget goes beyond its allocation.

Make all of the budget information available to those who authorize purchases and to the ones who determine purchases for the various areas of church work. They must see the importance of doing their part to meet the total financial challenge.

When a financial crisis comes in the middle of the year, figure the amount of money needed to meet the financial needs of the church for each of the remaining months of the year. Necessities are considered at this point rather than the amount allocated in the budget. The expenses must be cut back until the church is financially stable.

Establish a purchase requisition system for the church. Insist that purchase orders be obtained for all purchases and that any purchase of over $50 have two signatures.

Utilities. Telephone expense is often a large factor. Pay telephones can be installed. Check the telephone rate system now in operation in the church. Beware of having telephones available for general church use over which there is no control. Locks can be installed on the telephones.

The cost of light is often more expensive than people realize. Locks can be put on some of the switches in the church. Individuals should be assigned to turn off the lights. Smaller light bulbs can be installed. Urge people to turn off lights in rooms as they leave. Signs can be posted on light switches reminding people of light conservation.

Heat conservation is another factor. Are rooms being heated when not in use? Can the heat be lowered at times during the week? Check the window and door seals to make certain that heat is not escaping. Put locked shields on the thermostats so that unauthorized individuals cannot change them.

Several types of activities are very fine provided that there is money to do them. Suppers, breakfasts, farewells, and receptions enhance the friendly climate of the church. During the conservation period, those should be kept within the limitations of the budget and held whenever possible without the expenditure of church funds. Friendliness does not always have to be funded.

We must remember that there is just one set of pocketbooks. Money contributed to "pay-as-you-go" church activities is not available for budget support. Love gifts also drain from general support. Curtail offerings taken during church services for special features and speakers that are not part of the church budget. When such offerings are taken, they should be with the permission of the stewardship committee and go toward the budgeted funds.

What is internal control? It is a plan to not only detect error or fraud, but to safeguard assets; to check the accuracy and dependability of financial records and reports; to encourage operating efficiency and adherence to rules, regulations, and policies set by management. In a sense, internal control is the very basis on which the accounting system of the church is established.

Your congregation's internal control system can be greatly improved by accepting and implementing certain specific procedures. Different persons should count the offering, write checks, keep the individual contribution records, and reconcile bank statements. Separation of duties in that way greatly reduces the chances for misappropriation of funds and for error. At least two people should be in custody of the offering until it is deposited in a bank or placed in a night depository safe.

Offerings and all contributions received during the week should be deposited as soon as possible, just as for Sunday offerings. Offering envelopes should be distributed and used by all members. Reports should periodically be made of contributions. Any discrepancies should be reported immediately. Members should be encouraged to write checks rather than use cash even with an envelope system. Access to offerings should be limited to the head ushers. Access to the bank account should be limited to the treasurer.

Bank statements should not be reviewed by the treasurer, but should be received by the finance committee chairman and reconciled promptly by him from information provided by the treasurer. All checks should be signed by the treasurer or by him and one other person. The pastor should have no access to the bank account simply for his own protection. All payments should be by check. A check protector is useful. The church budget should be the basis for all expenditures.

Any variations should be explained, yet some flexibility is necessary. Expenditure control is virtually impossible without budget guidelines. Thus, the church budget is a very important internal control document. An audit should be conducted annually, either by a qualified audit committee or an outside auditor. All cash handling procedures should be in writing. A fidelity bond should be secured to cover those persons responsible for church finances.

Increasing Income

Remember that there are two sides to the coin. We must not only control expenditures, but strive to increase income. Inform the congregation week by week of the financial situation, and spend the Lord's money with care. Develop a friendly and positive climate within the church so that the people will feel like supporting the work. Call upon the church family to pray regarding the raising and spending of the Lord's money.

We can emphasize the importance and spiritual nature of offerings. That can be done by occasionally having an offering procession in which one member of each family presents the family's gift at the altar. Songs of dedication can be sung during the procession (preferably not the doxology, which is a song of praise and best suited to an entrance hymn rather than an offertory).

There are other ways to take up offerings than using money. Receive covenant notes written by people who wish to promise additional time, or dedicate their talents. Money could be eliminated and the collection simplified if everyone would use credit cards once a month instead of cash for their offerings. A regular transfer from one's bank account to the church's bank account is also possible.

Gifts of foodstuffs, cleaning materials, books, clothing for world relief can also be received in the offering. To involve more church members, have a different family each week serve as hosts (ushers) to greet the worshipers and pass the offering plates. Report finances in terms of work accomplished rather than dollars and cents.

Remember that we are offering, not collecting. It is an offering inspired by love, not appeasement or obligation. Christians recognize this as sacrifice. God performs miracles with our offerings. Our money supports and expands the ministry of the church.

An insurance underwriter can advise your membership on the best way to give life insurance to your church. It may be done by naming the church co-beneficiary of a policy, for example. You could encourage members simply to take out a new policy for the benefit of your church. In fact, you could organize a program in your church through which every member is encouraged to take out a $1,000 policy on his life naming the church a beneficiary. The member pays the premium and takes an annual tax deduction as long as he keeps up the payments. If he stops paying the premium, the church can take the cash value or a paid-up policy for the designated amount, or take up payment of the premium itself.

We should develop good motivation for giving. There are all sorts of motives for giving. One is guilt and another is fear. To motivate stewardship on the basis of guilt or fear is a real possibility—and some church leaders do it with notable success. We would prefer to motivate with grace and forgiveness.

Perhaps the lowest motive of stewardship is an attempt to bribe a "fickle" God. The worshiper brings his sacrifice and gift in hope that the giving of something precious to Him may induce God to treat him favorably or to refrain from harming him. Obligation is also a motive. That is prompted by the feeling David must have had when he cried in Psalm 116:12, "What shall I render to the LORD for all His benefits toward me?" That puts stewardship on the basis of a kind of commercial exchange. Another motive is sympathy. Many solicitations are made by the sight of suffering, which moves the compassionate person to act of charity and generosity. The appeal of world wide evangelism is also a motive that causes many to give liberally.

The strongest motive for giving is when the born-again Christian gives and keeps giving simply because it is an expression of his new spiritual nature.

E. F. Zeigler lists the following biblical motives for stewardship.[1]

1. Reward: to gain material blessing (Deut. 8:18; Mal. 3:10).
2. Law: to observe a religious law (Deut. 12:6; 14:28-29).
3. Justice: to manifest justice to our fellowman (Amos 5:24).
4. Duty: to recognize God and His Kingdom as having first claim (Matt. 6:33).
5. Stewardship: to discharge a responsibility entrusted by God (Gen. 1:28).
6. Faithfulness: to be faithful in this stewardship as God is faithful in all things (Rom. 12:8; 1 Cor. 4:2).
7. Worship: to give in worship is to imitate the Great Benefactor, God (Gen. 4:3-5; 8:20).
8. Consecration: to identify one's self with a need (Acts 20:35; 2 Cor. 8:1-5; 9:7).
9. Love: to love God in giving as God loved the sinner through Christ (John 3:16-17).

We should see offering as our commitment to mission. God gave us all; He expects all in return. Neither money, nor abilities, nor time can stand alone as a full offering. That goes for clergy and laity alike. Dr. Raymond Olson has written that "Christian stewardship is the response of the Christian to God's love and purpose, the recognition that he is appointed by God to use his life responsibly, productively and thankfully. This is his stewardship because Christ died for him. It is possible because Christ has risen."[2]

Hiring a Church Administrator

More churches are hiring church administrators in search of more efficiency in administration. Robert N. Gray has published a booklet entitled *Church Business Administration*. Anyone who is interested in this aspect of church activity should write to the Phillips University Press at Enid, Oklahoma to purchase a copy. Some of the general areas of responsibility for such an office would include finance, insurance, management, public relations, purchasing, contracts, administration, development, and taxes.

A congregation that employs a full-time business manager can delegate the responsibility for supervising financial operations to him. He in turn is responsible to the financial secretary for one phase of his work and to the church treasurer for another phase. On the other hand, the business manager is charged with the responsibility of supervising the office workers who actually perform the specific details of counting and accounting, recording information, and preparing financial reports.

Careful attention must be given to providing adequate safeguards to protect church funds. Obviously, the people who handle church money should be reliable and trustworthy. Besides restricting financial responsibilities to reliable people, the church should provide a definite system and plan for handling the money and records.

There should always be at least two people present when plate offerings are counted or when envelopes are opened and the primary records are prepared. The counting and preparing of initial reports should take place as soon as possible after the offering has been received. Ideally, it should be done right after each church service. However, because of time pressures, that may not be practical. It may therefore be necessary to place loose offerings and unopened envelopes into a special bag provided with a lock and keep it in the church vault or place it into a bank night-deposit vault to be counted at a later date.

As soon as the money has been counted and the necessary records made, a bank deposit should be prepared. Receipts should be deposited intact. No bills should ever be paid directly out of receipts.

As a further safeguard, churches can avail themselves of two kinds of insurance. 1) They can be insured against theft or burglary. That protects them against misappropriation of funds by outsiders. 2) The people of the congregation who handle church money should be bonded. That provides protection in the event of misappropriation of funds by them. A fidelity bond may list the exact name of each person who is authorized to handle money, or it may designate specific offices or positions that are covered, or it may give "blanket coverage" for all people who are authorized to handle funds without naming any of them. The first of those bonds is the least expensive but also the most inflexible; the last is the most expensive but also the most flexible and the widest kind of coverage. As a final safeguard, the congregation should make provision for regular audits of records and financial activities.

It is good practice for a church to issue receipts for all money it receives through channels other than the regular Sunday morning envelope or the loose plate offering. Such receipts should be prepared in duplicate, the original going to the donor and the duplicate remaining with the financial secretary. Some accountants suggest that donor envelopes be kept as long as four years as a source for verifying possible discrepancies. But there seems to be little justification for keeping them beyond the period of time when a report has been issued and the donor has been given a reasonable period of time (thirty to sixty days) to bring discrepancies to the attention of the financial officers.

The bank account in which church funds are kept should, of course, be an account in the name of the church and not in the name of an individual. A single bank account is preferable to several accounts for different funds.

Centralized Record Keeping

It is highly desirable to centralize all financial operations and keep all financial records in the office of the church treasurer. If the treasurer needs help, he should be given secretarial or clerical assistance. That is better than having individual departments and organizations of the congregation handle the banking of their own funds. Under such a centralized system assurance must be given to each society and department that it can conduct its business without being dominated by the treasurer of the congregation. In other words, the church treasurer serves as a banking service for the various organizations. He does not have authority to control the activities of societies and other church organizations.

The finance committee oversees the financial affairs of the

church. It supervises and approves the collection and expenditure of all church funds. It may delegate authority to approve expenditures that are made in accordance with the budget allocations. It approves the procedure and systems of accounts used by the treasurer and financial secretary. It has a responsibility to insure proper safeguards for all church moneys. It establishes procedures for the annual development of the church program and budget. Periodic reports are to be made to the boards and church membership when needed. It is that committee that develops and recommends canvasses for pledges and ways to meet unforeseen financial needs.

The program and budget committee leads the congregation in identifying the purposes and objective of the church. It evaluates and coordinates the program proposals of the several departments and organizations. It is their responsibility to try to determine the potential of the congregation. That committee presents the program and budget to the congregation for consideration, discussion, and approval.

The treasurer is under the finance committee and receives, records, and deposits all moneys of the church. He expends the church money in accordance with the authority delegated to him. The treasurer should render a monthly report of the status of the treasury and of the expenditures made against the budget. He should arrange for an audit of the church financial records each year. It is his responsibility to arrange for bonding for himself, which will be paid for by the church.

The financial secretary is under the supervision of the finance committee and is responsible for maintaining a record of all remitted pledges, contributions, and offerings. A separate account should be kept for each contributor. At least annual reports should be rendered to all contributors on record. All information concerning individual contributions and contributors is to be guarded information.

NOTES

1. In Richard V. Clearwater, *Stewardship Sermonette* (Findlay, Ohio: Dunham, n.d.), p. 75.
2. In Manfred Holck, Jr., *Money and Your Church* (New Canaan, Conn.: Keats, 1974), p. 66.

CHURCH NAME
Address
City, State, Zip Code

PURCHASE ORDER

To _____   Number _____

_____

_____   Date _____

We wish to purchase the item(s)/service(s) listed below. Please ship the purchase to the above address unless mentioned below.

    ____ A check for the amount of the purchase is enclosed.
    ____ Please bill us for the amount of the purchase.

Special Instructions _____

_____

Purchase Order Details

		Cost	
Quantity	**Item/Service Description**	**Per Unit**	**Total**
_____	_____	_____	_____
_____	_____	_____	_____
_____	_____	_____	_____
_____	_____	_____	_____
_____	_____	_____	_____
_____	_____	_____	_____
_____	_____	_____	_____
_____	_____	_____	_____
_____	_____	_____	_____

Total Cost $_____

AUTHORIZED BY _____

Distribution: Vendor—Numerical File—Open/Paid Vendor File

MONTHLY PERSONAL VEHICLE USAGE

Date: _____ Expense Code: _____ Amount: $_____

Submitted by: (Printed Name) _____

(Signature) _____

Approved by: (Signature) _____

Date	Purpose of Trip	Speedometer Reading		Miles Driven
		Starting	Ending	

Total Number of Miles _____

Amount due Individual = # Miles (_____) x ___¢ = $_____

MINUS Amount due Bus Garage $_____

= $_____

NOTE: It may be convenient to leave this form in your car attached to a clipboard with a pen handy.

TRAVEL VOUCHER

Submitted by _____ Date _____

Purpose of Trip/Expense _____

_____

	Dates					
Expenses						TOTALS
Mileage (__¢ a mile)						
Tolls						
Parking						
Common Carrier*						
Taxi						
Motel/Hotel*						
Breakfast						
Lunch						
Dinner						
TOTALS						

Travel Advance: $_____ MINUS Expenses: $_____

EQUALS $_____ due (Employee) (Church). Exp. Code _____

Comments _____

_____

Signature of Submitter of Voucher _____

APPROVED BY _____ Date _____

*Attach receipt

INTERNAL PURCHASE REQUEST

To: Church Purchasing Agent

Date:

From: (Signature) _____

VENDOR _____

Vendor Address _____

_____

| | | Cost | |
Quantity	Item(s)	Per Unit	Total

Total Cost $_____

SPECIAL INSTRUCTIONS _____

_____

_____

_____

Scriptural Financial Guidelines

Thine, O LORD, is the greatness and the power and the glory and the victory and the majesty, indeed everything that is in the heavens and the earth; Thine is the dominion, O LORD, and Thou does exalt Thyself as head over all. Both riches and honor come from Thee, and Thou dost rule over all, and in Thy hand is power and might; and it lies in Thy hand to make great, and to strengthen everyone (1 Chronicles 29:11-2).

The wicked borrows and does not pay back, but the righteous is gracious and gives (Psalm 37:21).

Do not withhold good from those whom it is due, when it is in your power to do it. Do not say to your neighbor, "Go, and come back, and tomorrow I will give it," when you have it with you (Proverbs 3:27-28).

A man lacking in sense pledges, and becomes surety in the presence of his neighbor (Proverbs 17:18).

There is precious treasure and oil in the dwelling of the wise, but a foolish man swallows [all he has] up (Proverbs 21:20).

Do not be among those who give pledges, among those who become sureties for debts. If you have nothing with which to pay, why should he take your bed from under you? (Proverbs 22:26-27).

There is a grievous evil which I have seen under the sun: riches being hoarded by their owner to his hurt. When those riches were lost through a bad investment and he had fathered a son, then there was nothing to support him. As he had come naked from his mother's womb, so will he return as he came. He will take nothing from the fruit of labor that he can carry in his hand (Proverbs 5:13-15).

"Will a man rob God? Yet you are robbing Me! But you say, 'How have we robbed Thee?' In tithes and offerings. You are cursed with a curse, for you are robbing Me, the whole nation of you!" (Malachi 3:8-9).

Do not lay up for yourselves treasures upon earth, where moth and rust destroy, and where thieves break in and steal. But lay up for yourselves treasures in heaven, where neither moth nor rust destroys, and where thieves do not break in or steal (Matthew 6:19-20).

For all these things the nations of the world eagerly seek; but your Father knows that you need these things. But seek for His kingdom, and those things shall be added to you (Luke 12:30-31).

On the first day of every week let each one of you put aside and save, as he may prosper, that no collections be made when I come (1 Corinthians 16:2).

Now, brethren, we wish to make known to you the grace of God which has been given in the churches of Macedonia, that in a great ordeal of affliction their abundance of joy and their deep poverty overflowed in the wealth of their liberality. For I testify that according to their ability, and beyond their ability they gave of their own accord (2 Corinthians 8:1-3).

But if anyone does not provide for his own, and especially for those of his own household, he has denied the faith, and is worse than an unbeliever (1 Timothy 5:8).

Let the elders who rule well be considered worthy of double

honor, especially those who work hard at preaching and teaching (1 Timothy 5:17).

And if we have food and covering, with these we shall be content (1 Timothy 6:8).

Bibliography

Planning and Implementing Church Ministries

Argyris, Chris. *Management and Organization Development.* New York: McGraw-Hill, 1971.

Bonhoeffer, Dietrich. *Life Together.* New York: Harper & Row, 1954.

Burns, James McGregor. *Leadership.* New York: Harper & Row, 1978.

Cardijn, Joseph. *Laymen Into Action.* London: Goeffrey Chapman, 1964.

Cook, Jerry. *Love, Acceptance and Forgiveness.* Glendale, Calif.: Gospel Light, Regal, 1979.

DeBoer, John C. *Let's Plan.* Philadelphia: Pilgrim, 1970.

Drucker, Peter. *Management.* New York: Harper & Row, 1973.

Engstrom, Ted W., and Dayton, Edward R. *Strategy for Leadership.* Old Tappan, N.J.: Revell, 1979.

Gordon, Thomas. *Leader Effectiveness Training.* New York: Wyden, 1977.

Kaufman, Roger. *Identifying and Solving Problems: A Systems Approach.* San Diego, Calif.: University Associates, 1976.

Küng, Hans. *Truthfulness, the Future of the Church.* New York: Sheed and Ward, 1968.

Lindgren, Alvin J., and Shawchuck, Norman. *Let My People Go: Empowering Laity for Ministry.* Nashville: Abingdon, 1980.

———. *Management for Your Church: How to Realize Your Church Potential Through Systems Approach.* Nashville: Abingdon, 1976.

Mager, Robert. *Goal Analysis.* Belmont, Calif.: Fearon, 1972.
McGregor, Douglas. *The Human Side of Enterprise.* New York: McGraw-Hill, 1960.
Perry, Lloyd M. *Getting the Church on Target.* Chicago: Moody, 1977
———. *Churches in Crisis.* Chicago: Moody, 1981.
Rath, Gustave; Stoyanoff, Karen; and Shawchuck, Norman. *Fundamentals of Evaluation.* Downers Grove, Ill.: Organization Resources, 1979.
Schaller, Lyle. *Parish Planning.* Nashville: Abingdon, 1971.
Shawchuck, Norman. *Taking a Look at Your Leadership Styles.* Downers Grove, Ill.: Organization Resources, 1978.
Wilson, Charles R. *Sojourners in the Land of Promise: Theology, Planning, and Surprise.* Downers Grove, Ill.: Organization Resources, 1981.
Worley, Robert C. *Dry Bones Breathe.* Chicago: Center for the Study of Church Organization Behavior, 1978.

FINANCIAL CONSIDERATIONS

Atkinson, C. Harry. *How to Finance Your Church Building Program.* Westwood, N.J.: Revell, 1963.
Banker, John C. *Personal Finances for Ministers.* Philadelphia: Westminster, 1973.
Beall, Delouise. *Christian Stewardship.* Grand Rapids: Zondervan, 1955.
Bramer, John C. *Efficient Church Business Management.* Philadelphia: Westminster, 1960.
Brattgard, Helge. *God's Stewards.* Minneapolis: Augsburg, 1963.
Canoyer, H. C., et al. *Economics of Income and Consumption.* New York: Ronald, 1951.
Carlson, Martin. *Why People Give.* New York: Council Press for Stewardship and Benevolence, 1968.
Cashman, Robert. *The Business Administration of a Church.* New York: Harper, 1937.
Cohen, Jerome B., et al. *Personal Finance: Principles and Case Problems.* Rev. ed. Homewood, Ill.: Richard D. Irwin, 1958.
Crawford, John R. *A Christian and His Money.* Nashville: Abingdon, 1967.

Feldman, Francis Loman. *The Family in a Money World.* New York: Family Service Ass'n, 1957.

Feldman, Julian. *Church Purchasing Procedures.* Englewood Cliffs, N.J.: Prentice-Hall, 1964.

Gray, Robert N. *Managing the Church.* Enid, Okla.: Phillips U., 1971.

Gross, Malvern. *Financial and Accounting Guide for Non-Profit Organizations.* New York: Ronald, 1972.

Harrison, George W. *Church Fund-Raising.* Englewood Cliffs, N.J.: Prentice-Hall, 1964.

Hatch, C. W. *Stewardship Enriches Life.* Anderson, Ind.: Warner, 1951.

Holck, Manfred. *Accounting Methods for the Small Church.* Springfield, Ohio: Clergy, 1974.

Holt, David R. *Handbook of Church Finance.* New York: Macmillan, 1960.

Kantonen, T. A. *A Theology of Christian Stewardship.* Philadelphia: Muhlenberg, 1956.

Knudsen, Raymond B. *New Models for Financing the Local Church.* New York: Association, 1974.

Lasser, J. K., et al. *Managing Your Money.* New York: Holt, 1953.

Linamen, Harold F. *Business Handbook for Churches.* Anderson, Ind.: Warner, 1957.

Lindgren, Alvin, and Shawchuck, Norman. *Management for Your Church: How to Realize Your Church Potential Through Systems Approach.* Nashville: Abingdon, 1976.

McCartt, Clara Anniss. *How to Organize Your Church Office.* Westwood, N.J.: Revell, 1962.

McKay, Arthur. *Servants and Stewards.* Philadelphia: Geneva, 1963.

McMullen, John S. *Stewardship Unlimited.* Richmond, Va.: John Knox, 1964.

Neithold, Eugene C. *Church Business Policies Outlined.* Greenville, S.C.: Church Books, 1976.

Nygaard, Norman E. *A Practical Church Administration Handbook.* Grand Rapids: Baker, 1962.

Page, Harry R. *Church Budget Development.* Englewood Cliffs, N.J.: Prentice-Hall, 1964.

Peterson, Robert E. *Handling the Church's Money.* St. Louis, Mo.: Bethany, 1965.

Rolston, Holmes. *Stewardship in the New Testament Church.* Richmond, Va.: John Knox, 1959.
Rosefsky, Robert. *The Money Book.* Chicago: Follett, 1975.
Salstrand, George A. E. *The Story of Stewardship in the United States of America.* Grand Rapids: Baker, 1956.
———. *The Tithe: The Minimum Standard for Christian Giving.* Grand Rapids: Baker, 1952.
Schaller, Lyle E. *Parish Planning.* Nashville: Abingdon, 1971.
———. *The Pastor and People.* Nashville: Abingdon, 1973.
Taylor, Jack. *God's Miraculous Plan of Economy.* Nashville: Broadman, 1975.
Thompson, T. K., ed. *Stewardship in Contemporary Theology.* New York: Association, 1960.
Walker, Arthur L. *Church Accounting Methods.* Englewood Cliffs, N.J.: Prentice-Hall, 1964.
Walz, Edgar. *Church Business Methods.* St. Louis, Mo.: Concordia, 1970.
Werning, Waldo J. *The Stewardship Call.* St. Louis, Mo.: Concordia, 1965.

Relational Considerations

Bell, Donald A. *How to Get Along with People in the Church.* Grand Rapids: Zondervan, 1960.
Brandt, Henry R. *The Struggle for Peace.* Wheaton, Ill.: Scripture Press, 1965.
Burchett, Harold E. *People Helping People.* Chicago: Moody, 1979.
Carnegie, Dale. *How to Win Friends and Influence People.* New York: Simon & Schuster, Pocket, 1936.
Chafin, Kenneth. *Help, I'm a Layman!* Waco, Tex.: Word, 1966.
Collins, Gary. *Living in Peace.* Wheaton, Ill.: Key, 1970.
Franke, Carl W. *Defrost Your Frozen Assets.* Waco, Tex.: Word, 1969.
Gangel, Kenneth O. *Building Leaders for Church Education.* Chicago: Moody, 1981.
Getz, Gene. *Building Up One Another.* Wheaton, Ill.: Scripture Press, Victor, 1973.
Givlin, Les. *How to Have Confidence and Power in Dealing with People.* New York: Prentice-Hall, 1956.

Perry, Lloyd M. *Getting the Church on Target*. Chicago: Moody, 1977.
Rogers, Carl. *On Becoming a Person*. Boston: Houghton-Mifflin, 1961.
Sanzotta, Donald. *The Manager's Guide to Interpersonal Relations*. New York: Amacom, 1979.
Stalker, James. *Life of Christ*. New York: Revell, 1949.
Tournier, Paul. *The Whole Person in a Broken World*. New York: Harper & Row, 1964.
White, Wendell. *The Psychology of Dealing with People*. New York: Macmillan, 1946.
Wright, Milton. *Managing Yourself*. New York: McGraw-Hill, 1949.

MISSIONAL CONSIDERATIONS

Allen, Roland. *Missionary Methods: St. Paul's or Ours?* Chicago: Moody, 1959.
―――――. *The Spontaneous Expansion of the Church and the Causes Which Hinder It*. London: World Dominion, 1960.
Anderson, Gerald. *The Theology of the Christian Mission*. New York: McGraw-Hill, 1961.
Belew, M. Wendell. *Churches and How They Grow*. Nashville: Broadman, 1971.
Brown, Stanley C. *Evangelism in the Early Church*. Grand Rapids: Eerdmans, 1963.
Chaney, Charles L., and Lewis, Ron S. *Design for Church Growth*. Nashville: Broadman, 1977.
Collins, Phil. *Getting Your Church Growing*. Calgary, Alta.: Baptist Union of Western Canada, 1979.
Dale, Robert D. *Growing a Loving Church*. Nashville: Convention, 1974.
Fickett, Harold L., Jr. *Hope for Your Church: Ten Principles of Church Growth*. Glendale, Calif.: Gospel Light, Regal, 1972.
Gerber, Vergil. *God's Way to Keep a Church Going and Growing*. 4th ed. Glendale, Calif.: Gospel Light, Regal, 1973.
Green, Hollis L. *Why Churches Die*. Minneapolis: Bethany Fellowship, 1972.
Hesselgrave, David J., ed. *Theology and Mission*. Grand Rapids: Baker, 1978.

Hodges, Melvin L. *A Guide to Church Planting.* Chicago: Moody, 1973.

———. *The Indigenous Church.* Springfield, Mo.: Gospel Publishing, 1953.

Hoge, Dean R., and Roozen, David A., eds. *Understanding Church Growth and Decline: 1950-1978.* New York: Pilgrim, 1979.

Hudnut, Robert K. *Church Growth Is Not the Point.* New York: Harper & Row, 1975.

Jones, Ezra Earl, ed. *New Church Development in the Eighties.* Cincinnati, Ohio: United Methodist, nd.

———. *Strategies for New Churches.* New York: Harper & Row, 1976.

Jones, Ezra Earl, and Wilson, Robert L. *What's Ahead for Old First Church.* New York: Harper & Row, 1974.

Judy, Marvin T. *The Parish Development Process.* Nashville: Abingdon, 1973.

Kelley, Dean M. *Why Conservative Churches Are Growing.* New York: Harper & Row, 1972.

McGavran, Donald A., ed. *Church Growth and Christian Missions.* New York: Harper & Row, 1965.

McGavran, Donald A., and Arn, Winfield C. *How to Grow a Church.* Glendale, Calif.: Gospel Light, Regal, 1973.

Mead, Loren B. *New Hope for Congregations.* New York: Seabury, 1972.

Metz, Donald L. *New Congregations: Security and Mission in Conflict.* Philadelphia: Westminster, 1967.

Nevius, John L. *Planting and Development of Missionary Churches.* Nutley, N.J.: Presbyterian & Reformed, 1974.

Noyce, Gaylord, B. *Survival and Mission for the City Church.* Philadelpia: Westminster, 1975.

Pattison, E. Mansell. *Pastor and Parish: A Systems Approach.* Philadelphia: Fortress, 1977.

Potter, C. Burtt, Jr. *The Church Reaching Out.* Durham, N.C.: Moore, 1976.

Schaller, Lyle E. *Community Organization: Conflict and Reconciliation.* Nashville: Abingdon, 1966.

———. *Effective Church Planning.* Nashville: Abingdon, 1979.

———. *Impact of the Future.* Nashville: Abingdon, 1969.

———. *Parish Planning.* Nashville: Abingdon, 1971.
Schaller, Lyle E., and Tidwell, Charles A. *Creative Church Administration.* Nashville: Abingdon, 1975.
Winter, Gibson. *The Suburban Captivity of the Churches.* New York: Macmillan, 1962.

PROCLAMATIONAL CONSIDERATIONS

Davis, H. Grady. *Design for Preaching.* Philadelphia: Fortress, 1958.
Dudley, Carl S. *Where Have All Our People Gone?* New York: Pilgrim, 1979.
Dulles, Avery. *Models of the Church.* Garden City, N.Y.: Doubleday, 1974.
Edge, Findley B. *The Greening of the Church.* 5th ed. Waco, Tex.: Word, 1971.
Fisher, Wallace E. *Preaching and Parish Renewal.* Nashville: Abingdon, 1966.
Garrison, Webb B. *The Preacher and His Audience.* Westwood, N.J.: Revell, 1954.
Gilkey, Langdon. *How the Church Can Minister to the World Without Losing Itself.* New York: Harper & Row, 1964.
Hall, Thor. *The Future Shape of Preaching.* Philadelphia: Fortress, 1971.
Haselden, Kyle. *The Urgency of Preaching.* New York: Harper & Row, 1963.
MacArthur, John, Jr. *The Church, the Body of Christ.* Grand Rapids: Zondervan, 1973.
McCabe, Joseph E. *How to Find Time for Better Preaching and Better Pastoring.* Philadelphia: Westminster, 1973.
McGavran, Donald. *Understanding Church Growth.* Grand Rapids: Eerdmans, 1970.
Morrow, Thomas M.; Billington, Raymond J; and Bates, James B. *Worship and Preaching.* London: Epworth, 1967.
Nagy, Ervin Valyi, and Ott, Heinrich. *Church As Dialogue.* Translated by Reinhard Ulrich. Philadelphia: Pilgrim, 1969.
Perry, Lloyd M. *Biblical Preaching for Today's World.* Chicago: Moody, 1973.
———. *Biblical Sermon Guide.* Grand Rapids: Baker, 1970.

Perry, Lloyd M., and Strubhar, John R. *Evangelistic Preaching.* Chicago: Moody, 1979.

Pitt-Watson, Ian. *Preaching: A Kind of Folly.* Philadelphia: Westminster, 1976.

Quayle, William A. *The Pastor-Preacher.* Edited by Warren W. Wiersbe. Grand Rapids: Baker, 1979.

Raines, Robert A. *New Life in the Church.* New York: Harper & Row, 1961.

Randolph, David James. *The Renewal of Preaching.* Philadelphia: Fortress, 1969.

Steimle, Edmund A., ed. *Renewal in the Pulpit: Sermons by Younger Preachers.* Philadelphia: Fortress, 1966.

Woodson, Leslie. *Evangelism for Today's Church.* Grand Rapids: Zondervan, 1973.